Beyond the Horizon

COMPILED BY

MARIA MBANGA-MAZVIMAVI

R&S
Creativity

Edited by Ruth L. Snyder

Published by RLS Creativity Press

ISBN: 978-1-7382403-4-0 (paperback)

978-1-7382403-5-7 (Ebook)

1st edition 2024.

Dedication

I would like to dedicate this anthology to all women and girls around the world whose stories are still buried within. There is power in your stories and NOW is the time to share your story.

And to my late mother Jester Masuku Mbanga aka "Masalu" mama, gogo whose story was never written but could fill a thousand pages—I promise to write your story mama.

Contents

Introduction

Compiling the anthology "Beyond the Horizon" was a labor of love for me and is a gift to women and the universe. This anthology is not just a compilation of stories by women and girls from across the globe, but it embodies the pursuit of dreams, the courage to explore the unknown, and a call to conquer fear. It brings to light women's resilience, boldness, wit, grit, and perseverance.

The stories from these women and girls inspire us to look beyond our immediate surroundings and challenges, urging us to embrace the possibilities that lie ahead. Their stories symbolize the endless opportunities that await those willing to venture beyond their comfort zones and strive for something greater. These stories pay homage to those before us—they are a reminder that "Impossible" can be "Possible" as long as one has faith, determination, and the will to try and never give up.

By pushing past any perceived limitations and daring to dream, we can unlock new potential and discover uncharted territories of personal growth and achievement. "Beyond the Horizon" encourages us to envision a future filled with hope and possibility, motivating us to take bold steps toward our aspirations and ultimately realize our true potential, aspiring to be the best we are meant to be.

∼

Maria Mbanga-Mazvimavi is a Women and Girl Child Empowerment Advocate, Community Builder, Leader, Philanthropist and Motivational Speaker. She is the Founder of Woman and Girls Arise Zimbabwe, Hope for Her Global Canada, Hope for Her Global USA. She is a Published Author and has a podcast called Sisters Talk, Up Close and Personal with Maria where she interviews women from around the globe who advocate for women and girls' issues varying from Education, law and justice and women advancement. The Alberta Black Gold Philanthropist of the Year award winner is Zimbabwean born. A secondary school English Literature teacher and Banker by profession. After graduation she sought to serve in the most disadvantaged communities in urban areas. Because of her passion for the Girl Child, she became involved in the Girl Child Network and was active in the Girl Child Movement and Affirmative Action Movement in Zimbabwe. She set up girls and women empowerment platforms and spaces for women and girls. She created safe spaces for girls and women and made them believe in their ability and equality with men. She helped girls keep active and removed them from vices that had swallowed many brilliant children. A service she still provides today in the different communities and organizations she continues to work with and volunteer.

Maria migrated to North America 25 years ago to join her family in Dallas Texas USA, and later moved to Canada. Coming from an Education background with teaching experience, Maria believes that Education is the door to freedom, offering a chance to a brighter future. "I am a true disciple of home is best, but I believe my God willing, I am a better citizen alive and tomorrow will be able to help rebuild a better community for the children who are the future. I have a fairly chequered life that has been bordering on hope. A hope that has never died, a hope that never fades, hope, that whilst we are immigrants in foreign lands, will one day be treated equal and not as second-class citizens so that in turn we enjoy the dream."

Through the various organizations she runs, she hopes to support Education, Literacy development and Economic Sustainancy for women and girls. Maria sits on various boards of numerous organizations internationally. She is a founding Board member for the International Childhood Cancer Charity USA. Maria is the past Vice President for Edmonton Multi Cultural Coalition. She served for Alberta Junior Achievement for five years. She is an active member of the Women, Peace and Security Network and founding Board President for Roses Life Women Center Canada.

Nest of Fear

THE BLACK HOLE OF SEXUAL ABUSE
BY HATSUKI MURATA

I pushed the stroller hard. *Go faster,* my seven-year-old brain yelled, *but don't hurt your little brother.* The cold air hit my face, and I swiped at the tears with one hand. Men and women, walking up and down the city street in Japan near my neighborhood, seemed oblivious. *Don't any of you see that I'm scared? Why don't you help me?*

I ran to my house, parked the stroller, and lifted out my two-year-old brother. I opened the front door to let him in, and I rushed to my mother. My father set down his coffee cup, alarmed at my frightened face. I don't remember what I said. An older man had hurt me, and I didn't know why. Suddenly I was afraid and ashamed at the same time. In only a few moments, I had become lost and confused inside.

This was the early '70s, the national economy was booming, and my parents decided to open a small family restaurant in Tokyo. Family members were expected to help, so I grew up in that restaurant, surrounded by loving aunts and uncles. As an outgoing child, protected by family, I was fearless. Every day was an adventure for me, and I lived in joy. My mother took me to small restaurants for lunch and greeted the owners by name. We walked the Tokyo avenues, hand in hand, while we went on errands. People filled the streets, coming and going, shopping, doing business, and going to the nearby train station.

One day after school I asked my mother to take me to my favorite park, but neither she nor my father could leave the restaurant. She said, however, that if I knew how to get to the park, I could go. "But" she said, "you must take your brother." Back then, the practice of allowing young children to travel alone was not unusual. The Japanese, a trusting people who valued children, often permitted their young ones to travel alone, knowing that other kind adults would provide directions if needed.

Mom put my brother in the stroller. I smiled my thanks and maneuvered the stroller, which was almost as tall as I was, out the door. I headed for the corner, turned right, and waited for the stoplight to turn green before I crossed the street. I walked about a quarter mile to the park and moved the stroller close to the playground where I could see my brother as I played.

I noticed an older man in a light brown trench coat carrying a briefcase in one hand standing near the edge of the play area. *Looks like a normal man who just finished at the office and was walking home when he decided to take a short break at the park,* I remember thinking. I glanced at him but continued to play on the monkey bars, having fun with the other children. But I felt like someone was watching me. The uncomfortable feeling continued, and I decided to leave. But before I could get to my brother, the man in the trench coat walked up behind me, his voice soft and friendly. "Hello, young lady. You are very pretty."

Politely, I replied, "Thank you." Although I often laughed and talked with restaurant customers, this man was too bold, and I wanted to quickly get away from him. I grabbed the handles of the stroller and began to leave but he stepped beside me, talking.

"The sun is going down and it's getting cold. Come here and let's sit down." He bent down, picked me up, and put me on his lap. Then he put my brother in the stroller right in front of us. He covered my legs with his trench coat and said, "I will keep you warm, but my hand is cold. Can you help me?" Again, he didn't wait for an answer before he put his big, cold hand on my thigh. "There. This is the warmest place to warm my hand. Thank you! You are very nice."

I stared straight ahead. People were all around the park, walking and talking and smiling. I looked around, desperate to catch someone's attention to get help, but I simply didn't know what to do. As I felt his fingers move, I told him abruptly, "It hurts!" but he didn't stop.

"Oh, no," he said, "it shouldn't hurt! My daughters are about your age and they like this." His breath was heavy on my neck. Even with my young brain, I sensed he was lying and that I was in danger. In fear and anger, I screamed inside my head, *God, where are you?* But nothing came out of my mouth.

Finally, I told the man I had to use the bathroom. He let me go and, while I was using the toilet, sharp pain shot through my body. I was crying now, frantically thinking about how I could grab my brother and get away from this bad stranger who was waiting for me just outside the door. After a few minutes, I simply dashed out of the bathroom, told the man that I was hurting and that I was going home. I grabbed the stroller and ran. He yelled after me, "Meet me here at the park every Thursday, pretty girl!"

I don't remember the words I used when I told my parents, but I noticed that soon my aunts and uncles no longer looked at me. They all acted as if nothing had happened. I knew that I was lucky to be alive, but why were my relatives punishing *me* by not talking to me?

I never went back to that park.

My normal, happy childhood ended that day. I now walked with my eyes down, slouching, looking at the ground. I avoided eye contact with strangers. Once friendly with my classmates at school, I now kept to myself. And I stopped smiling. A dark shadow followed me, its voice haunting me daily. *You're dirty. You're damaged, and everyone knows it.*

My grandmother—my father's mother—suggested that I and my brother live with her on the outskirts of Tokyo where she could take care of us while my parents focused on the restaurant. I believe she knew what had happened to me, and she thought that her neighborhood would be safer. My parents granted permission.

Grandma loved helping me with my homework, and I loved living with her in this new town where nobody knew me. She watched over me carefully, and I felt safe and protected. Soon she enrolled me in an after-school class. About forty students—mostly elementary and a few high school students—met at the home of a retired male teacher a short distance from my grandmother's house.

One day, after I had finished my assignment, the teacher informed me that the schedule had changed and I was to come thirty minutes earlier the next day. When I arrived, I discovered that I was the only student there. The teacher smiled at me, picked me up, and hugged me, telling me that I was a very pretty girl.

I panicked. The same feeling that I had experienced in the park with the other strange man overcame me, but no one was around if I were to scream. The teacher talked about how we should have one-on-one time more often, and it seemed like a long time before other students came in. The teacher quickly put me down and, although I was glad to have been released from his grip, I felt that familiar darkness engulf me, and wondered if it was somehow calling to these men to come find me.

That night I told my grandmother what had happened and that I didn't want to go to that class anymore. Thankfully, she agreed with me. But, as I grew up and moved a few more times to different towns and countries, I was found each time by a predator. My thoughts pounded. *I'm not safe anywhere! I can't hide! Danger is everywhere!*

As an adult, I know that my experience was mild compared to some sexual abuse endured by other children. But pain caused by any kind of abuse opens the door to fear—fear that feels like a big, open hole in the heart. And in this place—the black, open-hole place—victims hide and build walls so that no one can come inside and stay there.

This is the "Nest of Fear".

Physically, we reside in the same world as other people, but mentally and emotionally, we live in a dimension filled with shame and self-doubt. We ask ourselves questions. *Why was I even born? What is real love? Why am I hunted?* And the inevitable, *What is the point of living?* By staying in this "Nest of Fear", we are affected physically. Shock from mental pain affects the body so that it doesn't grow properly. We awaken at night with stomach pain. We analyze everything, overthink situations, and become numb to love, joy, and laughter. I became jealous of other girls who could genuinely laugh. I desperately searched for someone to love who would love me back.

I was eighteen when I first married. My husband became abusive and I wondered if I somehow attracted abusive men because I had been molested. My husband also had been abused as a child and still he chose to repeat controlling behavior as an adult. Many nights I would lie next to him, crying quietly, not knowing what to do. Was this a case of victim-attracting-victim?

After nine years of marriage, he met another woman, and I realized I had to get out of the situation before he killed me. I took our three children and fled to my mother's place. She let us stay with her, helping with child-care while I worked. *Finally,* I thought, *I am out of the Nest of Fear.*

Not true. Constantly, I was looking over my shoulder to see if he was waiting to knock me unconscious and take the children. Before the divorce became final, my search for genuine love and protection led me to a church where I learned about Jesus Christ. I became a Christian and heard that I was to forgive anyone who had hurt me. I felt anger rising up. *How can I possibly forgive a man who hurt me for so long?* I didn't understand forgiveness; I simply wanted to run away from everything. But when I wanted to leave my newly-found faith, I discovered that Jesus wouldn't leave me. Becoming a Christian had given me a new way of living.

Once I accepted Jesus and listened to Him, I was ushered out of the Nest of Fear over the course of several years. Eventually I forgave my ex-husband, and he asked me to meet him at a coffee shop to talk. That day the abusive man who had hurt me for many years apologized. Afterward, we went our separate ways, but we were no longer fighting or hating each other. Peace had come to us.

Although I was abused many times, I learned that not all men were predators. When I was being abused, I was unaware that help was available to me. Today, although domestic violence is rampant, victims have formed into active organizations and are fighting back. These people, akin to soldiers on the front lines in battle, are like angels sent from heaven to assist domestic violence victims to get out and stay out of dangerous situations. They encourage women to fill the black holes in their hearts with love, support, and education so that they might fly successfully on their own.

Thank you, "Hope for Her Global" and "Women in Bloom International." You and many others fight to save one girl at a time. We are here together to fight this battle to free others from the Nest of Fear.

∼

Hatsuki Murata was born in Japan, came to United States when she was 13 years old, and did not know any of the English language. Her hope was to start a new life in United States and put the painful childhood memory behind her. To focus on learning the English language, she has put her story writing and art drawing aside. Her dream was to live her life happy in this land of freedom, but she became a victim of an abusive relationship in her first marriage. She felt a victim will always be victim. She reached out to Jesus who is her light and He strengthened her to face the storms.

In her mid 50's she faced a diagnosis of stage four breast cancer, and the doctor gave her 1 to 5 years to live. Hatsuki became an author, publishing her first book in 2021 — *Facing the Storm with Kokoro*. She is working on her 2nd book — *Fight with Smile* about her stage four cancer journey to motivate other cancer patients, and also started a children's book series *Sukorina* with her own illustrations.

Reflections of My Shadow

BY LYNDA BANJA

She is Strong
She is Fierce
She is Bold
She has walked through
The fires of life and
Random sparks won't
Intimidate her flame

He paces up and down.........the woman seems to be in serious travail.

"What is happening?" The man asks.

Everyone is curious. This visitor is taking way too long to arrive!

As the sun creeps over the horizon and the clear morning sets in at around 4am all seems quiet. Then suddenly loud cries of a wailing baby pierce the silence.

There is commotion in and out of the room.

It's a long pause......he shakes his head in utter disbelief..."Not again!" ....words from the dad followed by a request to see the child..... his anticipation was, as is the norm in every other African home, that it would be a boy......one to continue his lineage....one who would bear his name.

Finally the nurse makes the long awaited announcement – it's a girl.

The man seems confused.......does he celebrate?

Should it have been a boy?....But it's a girl....this is his first child!

Do I name her after my mother?

Can I hold her?

What do girls need?

I have to ward off guys from my compound going forward!!!!

"Sir you can now come and see the child."

His face lights up – he was more than elated!

In his local language – "Here is my mother," as he took her up in his arms.

She was a spitting image of him – "Her name is Maria."

He would peep at her court every morning to see her sound asleep and leave work early to rush back and play with her.

This is how their relationship grew over the years.

Being a first child and a girl, she grew up under the hawk-eyed watch of her two best friends; her parents...and no she didn't have it easy. If anything she was forced to grow up faster than others her age.

She always had to think on her feet with a constant polite reminder from both....... "How will you handle things in the event that you were informed that both of us had passed on?" Those values and virtues of being apt, hardworking, self-disciplined, honest, and reliant on God were instilled in her from an early age. Any slight indication of bad behavior was nipped in the bud at indication of emerging, with the African cane.

As an infant she contracted a serious strain of Asthma which threatened to take her life, but the pediatrician guaranteed her mother that she would outgrow it towards the late stages of her childhood. Her formative years brought nothing but joy to her father who always believed that she was destined for greatness based on her good school performance, nomination to leadership, and extracurricular activities such as current affairs on behalf of her school.

The tide however changed when she turned 12. An unusual gift began to emerge. At the onset no one took much cognizance of it.

She spent an unusual amount of time in prayer.

Her discernment was razor sharp.

Her focus was unreservedly clear;

Her professional career seemed unequivocally cut out; she wanted to be a lawyer.

The irony however was her gentle demeanor. One would never portend that one day she would be a legal practitioner.

She, however, remained focused and obtained the required scores.

Her dad remained who he was and instead thought she would make a good accountant. He opted to take her to the best college in town to pursue accounting and that is where their disconnect started.

She tried persuading him, but to no avail.

She then opted to start making job applications. Fortunately, she landed her first job which involved hawking knives and it was no mean task.

From the reactions she received—from shocked glances to people closing their doors on sight of her with the set of knives— she knew this career path though humble but had to take another trajectory another path but she had to get an alternative first.

The local dailies became her best bet and yes it did yield results; she got her first office job after a whole gruelling week of having to wait for the interview with the owner of the company. On the very last day —'Big brother'—that's what they called him, gave her audience. He was rather curious though; "I have been seeing you here the whole week. How can I help you?" He asked.

Finally she explained her application based on the advertisement that had been posted and after a series of questions well answered he opted to give her a chance.

On the flip side, she had dropped the accounting course and was now staying with her aunt.

This angered her dad. He tracked her down and requested her employer to relieve her of her duties. Her employer finding this strange, declined, reminding her dad that she was an adult.

He then opted to have discussions with her if at all a truce would be drawn where she insisted on pursuing the law undergraduate degree. After a lot of back and forth he conceded and yielded.

The law degree was to be taken at a campus outside Nairobi.

It wasn't an easy journey but this was her dream career and this just had to happen – she had to put her best foot forward and she did for the four years.

Things came to a screeching halt at the 11th hour just when she was about to graduate. A lecturer made unfounded accusations against her; her values and integrity would be put to the scales. Ultimately this was resolved with the dean in her favor.

Fortunately, she made it to the graduation list.

The next step was to build up to be called to the bar. In Kenya this is a one-year crash course, which she undertook, and was successfully admitted to the bar.

One may assume that with being a lawyer everything would fall into place—you get this big job and voilà you live life eating out of a big spoon.

That was unfortunately not her case but she would not trade any of the experiences for anything; the experiences built the platform to her character, personality and network.

The order of the day became volunteering from one role to another; first at a small-sized to a medium-sized law firm then to a not-for-profit entity, then back to a small law firm to a medium- sized law firm in a span of five years.

Each had its own intricacies—life skills 101 to learn and wisdom nuggets to sieve out in her personal journal.

Proverbs 18:24 talks of a man of many friends coming to ruin, but there is a friend who sticks closer than a brother. Friendship comes in many dimensions; our foremost friends are our parents, siblings, neighbors, and the community at large. She had her fair share of instances where she had to define all her relationships, especially with her introverted personality. She remained reserved on who she allowed into her space

At first, being the smart cookie that she was in her teenage years, her parents and her were sworn enemies only to in her later twenties to-date that they were the best friends one could ever have. They've "been there, done that," and as the old African adage notes, "What an old man can see while seated, a young person cannot see when standing." Be humble. Life may be tough, but a lot can be gleaned from older, wiser people. To top it all off, there is the parental blessing which acts as a covering and the Bible notes that honoring parents comes with a promise.

The best of friends to date were built during her high school and campus years—women who would literally bend over to make sure all went well with her. This clique she would fondly refer to as her tribe —Lilo, Liz M. CK, and Ms. Oyagi! Through thick and thin their unwavering support remained year after year through the good and the bad!

Women are said to be their own worst enemies. This however was not completely the case with her. In retrospect, some of the best and most valuable experiences she had were from women who spotted her and thought, "Well, let's give her a chance." From her law undergraduate supervisor to the destiny helper at another organization, to the lady who was her senior as she undertook her mentorship and opted to take her under her wing to walk her through the ropes of legal practice, the list is endless. The key thing is that she always maintained an open mind and had a teachable spirit and yes; she never missed out and made the very best of every opportunity.

Mentorship, there is nothing more impactful than being able to pour out and invest on others, she had the grace of mentoring quite a number of young people but had to learn along the way why many individuals had reservations to undertaking this and those who did imposed certain caveats.

She gleaned a lot from both professional and personal mentors but interestingly, she focused on a certain watch list she had created of phenomenally unique successful women. These same women are breaking corporate glass ceilings, attaining great milestones, setting the pace in their diverse career roles, and leaving ground-breaking legacies in the political, social, and economic environment. By way of example one cannot speak of African women legends without mentioning Graca Machel (South Afria and Mozambique), Chimamanda Ngozi Adichie (Nigeria), Ibukun Awosika (Nigeria), Ngozi Okonjo-Iweala (Nigeria), Ellen Johnson Sirleaf (Liberia), Fatou Bedsouda (Gambia)and Samia Suluhu the current sitting president of Tanzania, just to mention a few. What do these iconic women have in common one may ask. One word; Resilience—a resolve to succeed; which they actually have and each curved a niche in their area of specialization. These were her mentors by observation.

Patriarchy has unfortunately made it the norm in many African households that girls are trivialized and that boys are highly esteemed as they are considered key in continuing one's genealogy. All these African women remain undeterred in their resolve to succeed, and yes, they did!

What was this then that had been hindering her?

What could she do about it?

What timelines and who needed to be engaged to make things happen?

Relationships: our hearts as women are wired for nurturing. In the same breath there comes a time where this heart has to be "shared" out. Being in love is the best feeling ever—been there done that—but before you allow a brother to build a home in your heart, to avoid unnecessary heartbreak, engage the heavenly father to confirm that you will not be chasing the wind. This is indeed who God has for you, a man after God's own heart, to worship and pray to God together, your best friend and companion, and some day to be the father of your children. God's choice is best and doesn't disappoint. When things get thick between the two of you the 4th man will be at hand because your man, your king ....is his son and he 'll get to understand that for a woman (as the Toni Braxton song puts it) *"It's the little things that matter!"* The heart that's meant for you will always want the best for you! There will be times when you will have to let go of that person that you dearly love. If it's meant to be, then they will definitely be back; if not, then it never was meant to be!

In law we say that you cannot give what you don't have (nemodat quod non habet)—love yourself first and giving love to your significant other will flow seamlessly because you hurting them would be akin to hurting yourself.

"Pure love knows that only one thing is needed to please God, to do even the smallest things out of great love, love and always love." – St Faustina.

Every opportunity life presents to you, always give it your very best. You never know how in the scheme of your life it be of benefit to you or another.

Life does not always present everything as we want it, but it is all about us being intentional about making good of what it has dealt us. Some have it all smooth but God the creator always puts a 'bump' on it to remind us that all we are and ever will be is about Him.

Why the nostalgic note? That is how my journey has been. The only difference is on this one I made a conscious decision that in all circumstances, whether good or bad, my life would be anchored on God and prayer. He has not disappointed.

We are sojourners on this earth and unfortunately I have had to learn the hard way that it is only God who is permanent, constant, consistent, and faithful; Each person God places on your path has a purpose; people and opportunities are only for a season.

Greatness is your birthright.

Who are You to shine brighter than others?

Who are You to take a step forward when others are shrinking back?

Who are You to make others feel insecure with your greatness?

You are a child of GOD.

Take a step forward, shine bright, - inspire others with your light to their own greatness.

The only way out is to pray for guidance for each and every endeavor you intend to embark on and that was;

The reflection of her journey

The reflection of her walk

The reflection of her shadow!

~

Lynda Banja is a Governance lawyer and GBV/SRHR Consultant, Social-Entrepreneur, Global Mentor, an accomplished Facilitator, Speaker & Trainer, with expertise in Corporate Governance, Corporate & Commercial Law, Risk & Compliance, IP, Gender & Inclusion. She serves on diverse boards and committees both regionally and internationally.

She thrives in excellence and bringing the best out of others through various speaker and mentorship platforms. A community change agent who believes in an all-inclusive and embracing world especially on the thematic area of education through her social venture. Her personal and professional motto is 'making things happen.'

The Wisdom Tooth

BY CHINYERE KALU

The sun seems to be very angry today. Looks like it is baring it fangs on the children of men. Whatever our sins, it must have been considered grave by him. No one seems immune as we are all served different measures of discomfort. I got served with heavy sweats at every imaginable part of my body.

What with beads of sweat threatening to swallow me, appearing more frequently even after every wipe with what originally was a white handkerchief now turned brownish from frequent visits to my face and chest area. This regular journey of the hand to my face in a battle with the sweats has left it bare and devoid of the cakes and layers of foundation and MAC loose powder. Where the lined-eye brows usually are; now stands naked, leaving a bare face, free from all the external additives to natural beauty.

Unashamedly, the beads of sweat now form a little running river underneath my skirt. Trickling down like one who has lost the grip on his bladder. I start to wipe the little river running down in between my thighs. My handkerchief protests as it had swallowed enough liquid and cannot soak up more. I stylishly squeezed it, so as to bribe it to take in more of the sweats. It did, though the result was not so pleasant.

I continued the routine of squeezing and wiping.

"Are you okay? My lecturer, who was standing at the podium in front of the class doing his thing asks.

"Yes Sir, I am okay. Just that the heat is getting to me." I replied.

Not immune from my predicament, he continued, just then, as though suddenly deported to our planet, and able to feel our plight. He says, "It is very hot today. I can see some of you have stopped writing. And others have improvised and brandish all sorts of hand fans. It is no use continuing this lecture, I will see you again on Wednesday."

Packing his notes as he talked, the loose sheets haphazardly put back into a transparent blue file, he looks up and announces what many had been praying for in the past hour.

"Good day class!" He leaves the class as he unimprisons us all. The class Rep. runs to take the file from him in his stride. Together they make it out of the class, finally announcing our freedom from heat, sweat, hunger, thirst, and all manner of unmentionable discomfort and sicknesses.

Making our way to the student's mini market, imagining how we will relish our delicious lunch we increased our pace unconsciously as though looking to get the award of the First to Arrive. Here, there are several make-shift shades where students come to eat. It is cheap and affordable and manageable in terms of taste. You either eat here or you go to the high-end restaurants down by the Senate building.

Most students on a shoe-string budget would give a leg and an arm to secure a seat at any of these shades. There is endless jostling amongst the women and some male traders despite the high number of students who throng here to satisfy the craving of the worms in their stomachs. The merchants are seen still hustling to attract customers to their stalls. They call out to students to get their attention to their wares even when these are all conspicuously displayed.

I can't seem to stop laughing each time I am passing through these lines of shades when the owner tries to woo me too by explaining how delicious his food is when I can already see it. One had said to me as I passed by, "The taste of the food is in the eating. Don't pass me by! Come in and have a bit."

You will think a bit is for free, I had muttered to myself as I walked to my choice shade.

Just as we began to climb the hilly part in the market the mai-suya calls out

"Aunty, come and taste!" Cutting out a slice of barbequed meat, thrusting it in our direction.

"Hmm, this Suya looks and smells good," Tope observes.

"I am running away from meat," I replied, as we walked past the mai-suya stand, past the fruit-seller and into our usual spot—The roasted yam shed. This spot gives you a totally different choice of food. It is plainly roasted yam and peppered palm-oil sauce, done on an empty big pot, supported by massive stones, with a second layer of the pot filled with coal. A wire rack separates the coal from the dry yam. At this joint, students get their tummies filled for less.

"Ah! Aunty, Una don finish for today? The yam seller greets us with a decorated face of smile.

"Yes, we don finish," I replied, not in the mood for long pleasantries.

"Ah! Tope mi," she calls out to Tope.

"Good afternoon ma!" Tope greets.

"Una come out on time, today," she enthuses.

"Yes, the heat was too much in class. Everybody was sweating, even the lecturer, so he stopped before his time was up because many were uncomfortable," I explained.

"Abeg, give us yam." Placing our order, I went to clear the table for the long anticipated hunger-quencher. I washed my hands in readiness for attacking the food. The worms in my belly jubilated in anticipation of what was to come. The sauce came first and Tope scrutinized the "face of the sauce"ensuring that her darling "pomo" was the soft type. Then the plate of roasted yam arrived. We moved to attack. Just at the first bite, I shouted, cringing as though from a physical attack; my first bite of the yam had sent a piece into the hollow of a bad tooth. This in turn, sent a nagging and excruciating signal to the right side of my brain and the overall pain knew no description.

"What is it?" Tope asked surprised.

"Toothache," was all I could say.

"Oh! Sorry, you have to go and remove it you know." She sympathized.

"I would have, but the thought of the pain of removing it has kept me from doing so. Now, that I

can no longer eat comfortably, I am afraid I will have to deal with my fear at the dental hospital. I will go

tomorrow. This pain is unbearable now."

Thus, my daily ritual at school was ruined, I forced down a litre of Chi-vita fruit-juice in place of food.

~

I was the fifth person to get to the District Hospital Maitama the next day. I didn't need to wait any longer. The tugging at the veins to my head which left me with un-abating headaches had to come to an end. I have learnt in these past months of living with the pain that; "The fear of fear is the perpetuation of endless pain."

"Today this bad tooth has to be plucked out" I swore to myself. Emboldened by pain, I went through the normal process of register-ing. I sat in line for my turn. A little child was called; the mother stood to take him in, but the nurse stopped her and took the child from her. My heart sank.

In, the swing-door closed. The mother stood confused, unsure of what to do next. A little later, the child reappeared with the nurse, crying like one frightened and pained at the same time.

"If this child's tooth was removed in such a short while and he did not die, this tooth will surely go today. I won't die," I said reassuring myself.

In less than forty-five minutes, a total of five patients had gone into the tooth theatre, emerging with different dimensions of facial expres-sions of pains.

I waited patiently for my turn. In my restless state, I brought out a novel from my bag: *Cry, The Beloved Country* by Allan Paton. I tried to read, but my mind would rather criss-cross the happenings around me. Seeing the fruitlessness of bringing out the book, I decided to put it back. Just then, he passed; huge, tall, and fair walking into the corridor briskly like one with a mission. He stopped, greeted a patient here, touched a child's cheek there. Threw a glance at my book. He strode for the swallowing door.

A little above an hour later, he re-emerged and called out to a woman, sitting three persons away from me.

She resurfaced ten minutes later with the left cheek bigger than the right one. Five minutes later, she went to the waste basket, spat out the blood-soaked cotton-wool, and returned to sit still.

"God, when will I be called?" I asked with no intention of getting an audible answer.

A nurse emerged from behind the swallowing door.

"Ifeoma Adams," She calls out. I stared at her for some seconds before it dawned on me that, that was my name.

"It's my turn!" I was startled and confused at the same time.

My heart resumed its pounding rounds.

I said to it, "If you pound even harder than this and up to heaven today, this bad tooth must go."

I walked in. At the sight of the different equipment, my heart pounded even harder, almost jumping out of its place.

"Madam, please come!" A masculine voice called out from behind a large piece of equipment.

Just beside him, a young man sat under a machine, having what looked like sand paper rubbing his teeth.

Like one scraping the top layer of the teeth. This came with a strong chemicalized smell.

Forgetting my fears and purpose for being in this equipment intimi-
dating room, I relaxed, waiting for him to assign me to a dentist.

"Come this way please," he said in a very courteous and polite manner. I
handed him my x-ray on demand. He lifted it to a nearby light from a bulb.

"Hmm, this is a special tooth." He enthuses. "The last of the wisdom
teeth," He adds.

"Yes, that was what the nurse said." I concur. "She said it is difficult to
remove and so takes a longer time," I volunteered.

"Don't worry about that," he reassured.

"Nurse!" He calls out to one standing close to what seem like the most
dreaded machines in the room.

"Prepare her!" He orders.

My heart resumes it racing feats at the pronouncement of those
words.

"Whatever happens today is the end of this tooth ache." I restated my
commitment to myself, all in a bid to steady my racing heart. I had
researched about this problematic tooth and came to the knowledge
that it is called a wisdom tooth. One of the three molars. It comes out
late in life I remember vividly that this tooth came on at the age of
twenty–eight after the birth of my second son.

One wonders why it should grow out lastly and lately and still be the
first to be extracted. Anyway, whatever happens, it must go today, I
can't bear this pain any longer.

"Madam, lie here please." The dental assistant's voice brought me
back to the surgery room. Now very resolute. My heart stopped
pounding hard, or at least less audibly.

She fixed the operating light on my face. The chief dentist, came in, wearing his gloves, and began a conversation as he examined my mouth with the hand mirror. "How long has this tooth

been giving you troubles?" He asked.

"Over a year, I answered.

"Why did it take you so long to come?" He queried further. Then he injected the base of the bad tooth with what looks to me like the tiniest needle I have ever seen.

"I was afraid," I replied.

Collecting a plyer-like device from the nurse, he twisted the tooth as he continued his conversation with me. "We have only one department in the whole of this hospital where people are not afraid. You know the place?" He asked.

"No," I replied.

"It is the mortuary. That is the only place where people do not feel pain." He lectured, bringing out the bad tooth.

~

Chinyere Kalu is a World Pulse Digital Ambassador, Encourager, a Featured Vocal Contributor in story telling.

She has been working with women since 2016 and is the President of Glammy Mums Africa. She exposes women in their late thirties to the signs and symptoms of Peri-menopause.

A poet and the author of *No One Told Me*, a handbook for women.

A two time mentor of the Technovation South Africa competition to five girls teams.

A Toastmaster who holds a degree in Literature in English from the University of Abuja.

Living Life Royally

EMBRACING ABUDANCE AND GROWTH
BY KIM BULLOCK

Knowing you're birthed into greatness for a special purpose but not seeing the immediate results of your vision can be discouraging. I've been through a lot in life and learned some of life's most valuable lessons from tough situations. Most think it's when you're succeeding and winning that you learn the most. However, in actuality it's when your faith is tested, and trials occur when you increase your strength and wisdom. Everything from losing business deals to the loss of my late husband during the pandemic devastated me, and I became overwhelmed with grief and burdens, which took me off course temporarily to the destiny I need to fulfill on earth. I'm writing from my heart as I say this. Please never allow life's temporary challenges to distract you from serving in your Royal role and executing greatness through your purpose.

God hand-picked you Queen, to rise above all adversity and thrive abundantly in all your endeavors. Living life as a Queen is not about royal robes or thrones; it's a mindset that embraces abundance, growth, and the divine calling to be spiritual royalty. As God's finest creation, we have Royal blood running through our veins and are endowed with the potential to lead lives of purpose, prosperity, and influence.

Here are some of the keys to success I have used to elevate in life and overcome obstacles. Everyone wants to be successful in life and business, but there will be trials and tests God will put us through in order to elevate to the next level. Please take some of these tips that I have applied in my personal life and business to thrive past difficult times.

Tip 1: Cultivate a Heart of Gratitude

A Queen's heart is filled with gratitude. Start each day by counting your blessings, not your troubles. This shifts your focus from scarcity to abundance, allowing you to approach life's challenges with positivity and resilience.

Tip 2: Invest in Continuous Learning

Royalty never stops learning. Embrace a growth mindset by seeking knowledge and wisdom in all areas of life. Whether it's through books, mentorship, or new experiences, continuous learning fuels ambition and innovation.

Tip 3: Build a Legacy of Service

Queens serve their communities with love and strength. Find ways to contribute positively to the lives of others. This creates a ripple effect of goodwill and sets the foundation for a lasting legacy.

Tip 4: Balance with Grace

Like the Proverbs 31 woman, balance your roles as a wife, mother, spiritual leader, and businesswoman with grace. Prioritize your responsibilities and delegate when necessary, understanding that you can do anything, but not everything.

Tip 5: Foster Resilient Faith

Adversity is inevitable, but a Queen faces trials with unshakeable faith. Cultivate a deep spiritual connection that will anchor you during storms, reminding you that you are never alone in your struggles.

Tip 6: Embrace Your Unique Influence

You are created to be influential. Recognize and embrace your unique gifts and talents. Use them to inspire and lead others, setting a standard of excellence and integrity.

Tip 7: Pursue Excellence with Humility

A queen pursues excellence, not perfection. Strive to do your best while remaining humble. Remember, true royalty is not about superiority, but about serving with excellence and humility.

Thinking abundantly and living like a queen is a transformative journey. It's about embracing your divine identity, leading with wisdom, and walking in the abundance God has ordained. By following these seven tips, you can navigate life's complexities with the poise and purpose of spiritual royalty, creating a prosperous life that honors your divine calling. Remember, you are more than enough, and your reign is now.

~

Lifestyle and Abundance Coach **Kim Bullock** is a highly requested, results-driven Abundance Mindset Expert, Royal Protocol Spiritual Teacher, Elite Award-Winning Author & Coach, Revolutionary Leader, Founder and Advocate for the Ambitious Women Movement.

She serves entrepreneurial women and online influencers with abundance mindset coaching and royal protocol masterclasses to show up powerfully as Queen in their business and personal life.

Kim's powerful coaching sets her clients apart from the ordinary, by teaching her mentees to step into their God-given destiny by dismissing the bankrupt mindset, uprooting a poverty mentality, and embracing royalty as part of their spiritual DNA!

Allow God to Transform Your Mind

BY CHENNAI MBANGA

H ope exists for the one who is bold enough, brave enough and determined enough to grab hold of it. And you are all these things and more if you'd just give yourself a chance; if you'd just give this moment a chance. Where you are doesn't have to be the end of the story; exercise your creative power to change things according to what you want to see.

Suspend the thoughts that you have about the past. It's not the time to consider the lessons learned from the past, but it's time to run, untethered, un-abandonedly into your future. It starts today; not tomorrow, when the burden is lighter; not next month when the load becomes manageable; not next year when the economy might get better. Today. How many "tomorrows" do you have until they run out? Everything expires, even your own body. At some point, you will return to the dust from which you came; you, who can't even command your time right now, do think you can command death to wait?

You have time because you are breathing, and thinking, and considering, and hoping and dreaming. Every day is an opportunity for you to change the way you think about this current situation; an opportunity to rewrite the story of your life, rewrite the story of the person looking back at you in the mirror. Hope doesn't cease because you have given up on yourself.

Without a doubt, there are environments that make it seem as though they will destroy you and every good thing you attempt to do. And certainly, there are people who exist to steal and destroy blessings—cut off opportunities, snatch the choicest things out of our hands—before we even discover what they are, and what we can do. There are parents who birth children that they devour. Their children are like a blood sacrifice—when they are ripe, full of potential and opportunity—they become prey to their teeth. If they don't consume their children's expectations, they frustrate them and scatter every good thing. There are wicked parents, wicked partners, wicked siblings, wicked friends, wicked acquaintances. They are like a deadly poison that's undetectable. All you have are unexplainable symptoms of lack, of stagnancy, of frustration, but the source is hidden in plain sight; packaged inconspicuously.

Understand this: your hope and your faith are your greatest assets in such circumstances. If you believe there is better than where you are; if you conceive in your heart that things will change, can change, must change, then by God they will. If you decide to strengthen your mind, strengthen it by the power of the word of God. Be anchored in Him whose existence cannot be fully articulated nor subdued.

Surely, people can destroy by their words; and by their words they can mend and create. Your hardship doesn't make your words ineffective. They are just as potent, if not more, in your times of travail.

It sounds gimmicky, as though it's a luxury enjoyed by those who have never experienced hardship. But why is it that when your mind is clear you are able to see possibilities; you're able to see the value of what you have and make use of it. When your mindset changes, the door to possibilities is opened. Your environment has not changed, your skill level has not changed. Your bank account has not changed, but when that shift happens in your mind, and is wholly accepted by your heart, you have escaped imprisonment. Physically, everything may still look the same; but that mental liberation will soon manifest physically.

As I have said, change the way that you see yourself, who you are, what you are capable of.

You must decide that your life has value and worth. God is not wicked, that he would allow you passage into this world, only for you to die at the works of his creation.

Decide that the purpose that you are created for must be accomplished. Decide that you did not enter earth to be a sacrifice to wickedness. Decide that no matter what, you will make it in this life. Decide that your aspirations are worth pursuing; that your life is worth investing in. Decide that your desires are worth exploring and bringing to fruition. Decide that, come what may, you will be fruitful. Decide that there is room for you; decide that there is room for your future generations. Do not take on the fear of those who have concluded that there aren't enough resources for everyone.

Every day there is someone giving up their territory, their dominion given to them by God. Every day, there is a lie spun and a lie believed. However, it is also true that there is someone out here breaking out of a prison, taking hold of the promise, fulfilling their purpose, and living a life that their imagination could not have conceived.

If you don't decide what is possible, someone will decide for you. If you don't decide that you are worth it, someone will determine your worth and value; if you don't fight for yourself, someone will fight you, and take from you. If you choose not to wake up; someone else is happy to keep you blind, ignorant, and foolish. If you don't draw the line, someone else will determine your boundary lines for you.

Wake up. Change the way that you think about yourself. Change the way you think about what is possible. The Bible says *"Be ye transformed by the renewal of your mind"* (Romans 12:2). Transformation doesn't precede the renewal of the mind. The mind must be renewed first so that the channel for transformation is opened. Your mind, the seat of your soul, must be rehabilitated: your thoughts, your perspective, your self-esteem. Thoughts that allow you to be in survival-mode, are not the thoughts that'll allow you to be fruitful in your new level.

Lean into the liberty before you.

There is liberty available to everyone. But it will take those of us who arise, and decide that our circumstances will not rule over us; they'll not destroy us, they will not overcome us. For a little while you may have cowered, but soon, the fear of you will be upon all those who made you afraid.

You are bold enough, brave enough, and determined enough. So, renew your mind. Allow God to transform your mind, and then allow Him to transform the world through you.

❧

Chennai Mbanga was born in Zimbabwe but has spent most of her life in Canada. Writing has always been a passion and a comfort, and she cannot remember when she began writing, but it's something that has carried her through many journeys. Chennai's writing is infused with her faith. It's through faith that she has gained courage to love writing, explore calligraphy, and pursue learning new languages. As a writer and a woman of faith, words are powerful, and she's gaining an understanding how transformative words are. Chennai desires to build others through words, that they may stand confident in who God purposed them to be.

Here for a Reason

BY TAMARACK VERRALL

I am told that I was born yelling. I have known for a long time that that I am here to end violence against women and girls, globally. So, it makes perfect sense to me that I was born yelling.

When I was eleven my mother had surgery because she had lost a baby she was carrying. She knew for months that the baby was not alive but she was forced to carry a dead foetus at risk of her life. She had to wait for three male doctors to agree. They operated on her on Valentine's Day. I was aware that she could have died. My mother had no access to the family bank account. Only men could access money. She needed my father's signature for her children to get medical help. We were six active children. Most women in this world have no access to medical care.

My mother loved nature. She made sure that we went camping every year. In the 1950's we swam together in lakes clean enough to drink. Now lakes across Canada have poisonous toxins seeping in, buried in the earth around them by rich companies, especially on land where

Indigenous people live. The same land that my forefathers invaded and began to ruin, the bloodthirstiness still in them from the times their fathers burned women as witches, my ancestresses, particularly if the women were healers.

My mother insisted that my five brothers and I share house cleaning and dishes. She quietly resisted what was taught in the wider world. I grew up encouraged to find within myself what I'm here to do with my life. My mother's love for our planet and her sense of fairness created my awareness of what needed to be done as an environmentalist and as a feminist.

When my friends were raped as teenagers my life purpose galvanized into ending violence against women as a first essential first step toward a world of no violence, a humanity living in harmony with each other. I searched for books by women, gathering pieces of information on what women have done in the past. I was consistently told that women had never done anything worth writing about. I hated studying history, memorizing dates and reasons for wars. I knew there must have been a very different story.

At sixteen I was next in seniority to be assistant manager of the local swimming pool. The job was offered to a junior lifeguard. I contested and won. My first feminist victory, in this global community that keeps women working for no money in a vile money system.

This was a time in North America when a progressive movement was growing within the art community with the Beat Poets. I came into my early adult years in the 1960's as the hippy generation grew, and alongside it our growing women's movement. The heart of my work has been my determination to end all forms of violence against women and girls, essential to living peacefully and respectfully on this earth as a global society. Violence from men of every political leaning galvanized our intention.

As young women we were well aware of violence against women and girls and of years of broken promises that the violence would end. We learned that generations of women had been challenging these warring male governments on their control of the world for centuries. What was hidden were stories about peaceful societies in which women were and are respected leaders. We challenged the laws that legalize discrimination against women. We challenged the inability to end wars and this money system, dependent on free labour by women and people still in slavery. We looked into the hidden women's history, stealing women's inventions and discoveries. We challenged the erasure of women's leadership and the evidence of peaceful times. I promised myself time to study this evidence of times and places in which women were and are respected leaders. The women I turn to are women who have been documenting this for years.

I hold in my heart my ancestresses, tortured and burned as witches not long ago. Ceremony honouring ancestresses is deeply rooted in me, ceremony for healing, and working with women who know we were born to create these changes and these healing oases. We realized we knew instinctively how to offer healing. Movement, dance and nature give me clarity and the strength to pay attention to where violence occurs, and to continue to work for change.

In the 1970's in the city I grew up in, one doctor provided abortions despite being jailed at one point for 18 months. A group of us opened one of the first women's centres, in part to provide support for women arriving in need of abortions, from parts of Canada and globally. We met to identify and document the discrimination against and violence toward women and girls. Women studying to be doctors wrote the *Birth Control Handbook*, and we distributed it illegally to women who were not married. We were inspired as we searched through history for what women had done before us, forming contact with other groups and realizing women were gathering in many places.

We worked together to end violence, to end poverty and to take care of this Earth.

We were met with walls of resistance to women getting access to money. We learned how to meet in circle with each other and how to build a women's movement, inspired by the news that this was happening in many parts of the world. We created networks, travelling to meet in person, some of us travelling widely, searching for women working for change. We were determined to build a global movement. Within our small women's centre we listened to women's stories and realized the importance and the healing power of bringing women together to talk, to heal and to build this new wave of a women's movement. We were ridiculed, just as we are now. We knew the importance of lifting the voices of women, freeing our thinking, speaking out about the lies being taught.

We created plans for a future in which every woman is free, respected, and safe. We researched our herstory, the story of women and of our resistance to patriarchy, intentionally hidden from us. This information is deeply precious to me, protecting it and making it known so that it is not lost again. I am grateful for our herstorians who have dedicated their lives to researching women throughout time.

When we could, we traveled to meet. We learned from each other how to produce women's newspapers, open centres and bookstores, teach healing arts and self defense. We shared books by women, accomplishments by women, information kept from school curriculums for challenging the intentional manipulation of knowledge. We continued to call for peace and the end of all control over women.

Through women's centres, healing centres and shelters we provided places for women and for girls to talk together and heal from the violence. We learned that throughout time women's circles have been an integral part of communities. We were grateful to be meeting as women who know that the purpose of our lives is to work for change. We celebrated that there were many of us, women writers, speakers, and creators of the 1970's Women's Liberation Movement, the Peace Movement and the Environmental Movement. We were inspired by women who had opened the paths. We built connections and planned. We shared our passion to end all violence against women, to end all violence everywhere, including the violence against our beloved Earth. I travelled across North America, Europe, North Africa and India learning and believing that women everywhere were looking to find each other, share information, and create change.

In the 1970's I had a recurring dream that I did not want to marry, despite gentle and aware men in my life. In this dream I would agree to marry, feel an imposing dread, run out of the ceremony, jump into a red convertible car and head for the woods. By 1973 I had embraced my lesbian self, and attended a camp of feminists organized by the Red Stocking Women in Denmark. Within the lesbian community I found close conspirators, fearlessly determined to create a world in which all women are free.

Maligned for the work we do to offer female only space for discussion and healing, maligned for not marrying a man, we are doing what we are here to do. Nothing will stop us. We are still working together today.

Government inaction on ending the violence has been chronic and deliberate. The violence continues and escalates in new forms, directly aimed at those of us who write, speak, and create events for women. We are called troublemakers, discredited, and silenced.

Many of us travelled as widely as we could to meet, share stories and information, writing for women's newspapers and magazines, hosting each other to speak. We continued to meet in circles to heal, to help each other heal and create change. Women's Centres are our home bases.

I was one of many setting up these centres, strengthening ways to find and stay in touch with each other, raise our voices, and meet to discuss needed change. I was determined to use my voice and to challenge the governments. The UN Declaration of Human Rights was signed the year before I was born, created by women, notably Hansa Mehta from India, Minerva Bernardino from the Dominican Republic, and Begum Shaista Ikramullah from Pakistan. We were not taught this in school. The hidden information about women is what I live to bring forward. The healing and leadership of women is what I live to see happen.

In Vancouver in the 1980's I set up groups for girls through Social Services. They had stories of sexual violence to tell. I planned to do the same when I moved to Ottawa. A newspaper article warned that a lesbian was setting up a group for girls implying that I was dangerous. The Children's Aid Society of Ottawa defended me. I was donating my time, as so many women do. A conservative group tried to have me fired from my paid job. Trying to get women fired is a common attack but it didn't work.

What was important was to offer time together, helping each other heal, believing in each other's ideas, learning where the emergencies were, speaking together about ways to create a global society with no violence, while in the grip of an immoral system of ongoing brutality toward women, and never-ending wars.

This is what we use precious moments for. To witness a woman believe in herself, often for the first time. I have been grateful to know so many others working to solve these emergencies, end the wars, trafficking, slavery, and poverty, while empty government promises of freedom for women and girls continue and while women working for these changes are punished. As violence and control over women continue in ever new forms, we continue to find each other and work together. This is where my heart is. My work is focused. We carry and repeat what we know about women throughout time, and about times in which women's leadership created peace. We carry this in our bones.

On Healing

For years I have been deep in this women's movement, grateful that we are finding each other in great numbers. I have long been surrounded with women who live to create these changes needed in our world. Many of us are lesbians. Many are healers. I was aware long ago that I can heal through discussions, through loving and caring. I learned ways to keep myself as strong and as clear as possible and have been able to watch this movement grow. Our herstorians continue to find and document women leaders of the past, images of women in ceremony with drums, women being approached with respect for advice, and we recognize the healing circles. I knew that this was what I could offer, to bring women and girls together to heal, to learn and repeat stories of our past so that it can be known.

My adult life has been in cities, travelling or in the woods. I have always been part of our growing women's movement, demonstrating, speaking out, writing to government officials, meeting with other women strengthening, working together, travelling to speak and offer workshops, share writing and ideas. For ten years I was able to enter the federal prison for women in Canada to meet regularly with most of the women. I was sent across the country twice to strengthen services for women upon their release and to meet women housed in the provincial jails, to listen to their stories. I also worked in a half-way house. I worked for prison reform and a stronger network of support in the community. These women had survived so much violence and many are now strong, dedicated leaders in their communities.

My Source

I have always loved gardening and the woods, especially trees. I have learned about the love our ancestresses had for land, and how many were healers in the woods, the first to be attacked. I lived on three different lands, part of a network of women's lands and for twenty years was an organic farmer. I met many women farmers. We offered time in the woods for women wanting to gather strength or plan together within the women's movement. Discussions. Teaching. Writing. Theatre. Music. Financial survival. We called for paid work for women globally, for women tending to all these emergencies, constantly and still today with little to no funding.

Urban Women's Centres and Women's Lands spread across the continent. Networks grew. We continued to dream of women rising, globally, respected for our call for a direction forward peacefully together. From my first cry on entering this world I had found my way to speaking out, writing, planning, demonstrating, and forming deep connections with others on the same path. I celebrate younger women having access to our herstory. I question why it is being demonized.

A woman who knew me well gave me *World Pulse* in magazine form for my 65th birthday. I found the news that never gets reported. So many women speaking out and working with each other globally, all gentle people included, working for a world together in which we are in harmony with each other and our planet. Moving forward together committed to ending violence against women and girls, valuing women's leadership, undoing the suppression. *World Pulse* has become my home. Even describing that *World Pulse* exists creates powerful hope. I jumped in deeply, and discovered a community now 80,000 from 227 countries, led by women, unapologetically focused on ending all violence against women and girls, working to raise women's voices for change, challenging the global economy built on free labour of women, trafficked and enslaved people, while long ago promises of change continue to be broken. All this and the chance to be in direct contact with each other and working together. On my 65th birthday I joined online.

When I emerged from the woods I drove across Canada, meeting and reconnecting with women's groups, strengthening ties, bringing news of how we are now working together globally through *World Pulse*. I live in a city and continue to meet with my sisters in the woods when I can. My hope lies in the potential we have through all of the organizations that unapologetically raise women's voices and create pathways for our work.

As I continue to find ways to offer healing, to learn and speak out about our past, stay close in touch with women globally and stay strong through time in nature, I have grown into the grassroots leader and healer that I am today.

∿

Born in Ottawa, Canada, raised in Montreal **Tamarack Verrall** has lived in Vancouver, Ottawa and in the woods farming, returning to Montreal in 2014. Her travels have taken her across Canada, the USA, parts of Europe, North Africa, India, New Zealand, Mexico and Tobago. Tamarack's work has spanned teaching, public speaking, writing, counselling and healing work with women and girls. In 2014 she discovered worldpulse.org enabling work with women in 227 countries. In 2020 Tamarack was awarded the first World Pulse Spirit Award and she currently serves on the Steering Committee. She lives to see women respected and free.

Voices in a Shadow

ECHOES OF MENTAL HEALTH AND WELLNESS
BY PRISCILLA MUNEMO

Every day tragic stories of someone with a mental illness are told on the TV: gruesome brutal murders, rape cases, and horrific suicidal events are reported. News on wars, pandemics, earthquakes, tornadoes and so much more has brought in times of crisis and uncertainty while the mental health of individuals has been forced to the brink of collapse. These pressures have come along with stress, anxiety, panic attacks, depression, and worsening pathologies such as Bipolar, Schizophrenia and more. However, stigma has always been the stumbling block surrounding mental health, hence the persistent biases have been a tripling factor on the already accrued distress. Therefore, mental health is an important topic that needs to be treated with primary concern. Mental health deserves to be given a chair at every table, in the home, at school, in the church, in the workplace, at every meeting platform so that discussions on mental health are normalised and become beneficial to every individual and the rest of the society. Consequently, increased, and continuous effort must be channelled towards treatment options, methods and modes of delivery that are in line with technological advancements.

STIGMA is a shameful story that has anchored the bias towards mental health. Often in societies mental illness is something that has been witnessed. For some it has been a reality in their families—they have played roles of caregiving—whilst to others it is something they are live with every day. Sadly, to many, mental illness has remained an untold story concealed within their walls. On several occasions the media has been awash with mass shootings in shopping centres, schools, halls. News has been reported on gruesome, brutal murders that have left communities gutted and many distraught. But could these countless stories be attributed to mental illness? Could they be cases of untreated mental illness? What if society could take pro-active steps to prevent these tragedies from happening rather than waiting and taking reactionary steps? How could we do this? The answer lies in you and me. Its time to step up, talk, and walk the part on mental health at every platform, normalising mental illness and breaking the bias by seeking early treatment and help.

The World Health Organization (WHO) defines mental health as a "state of well-being in which an individual realizes his or her own abilities, can cope with normal stresses of life, can work productively and is able to make a contribution to his or her community." The onset age of mental illness varies across pathologies. Many affect children from birth right through teenagerhood up to adulthood. Research records that 1 in 5 American children and youth between the ages of three and seventeen, have a diagnosable mental, emotional, or behavioural disorder. What worsens the matter is that over 80% of those children are not receiving treatment (Child Mind Institute), hence these conditions degenerate to adulthood affecting one's life experiences including school, social life, and success. The risk posed attributes to severe life challenging experiences such as physical ailments, like cardiovascular diseases, cancer, worsening pathologies like schizo-phrenia, bipolar, depression and defunct social action like involvement with the criminal justice system. Therefore, this means parents need to be conscientized about mental illness, identifying irregular mental, emotional, and behavioural problems in children to seek accorded help. Teachers in schools also need to be child sensitive. Schools must capacitate teachers in this regard so that teachers can teach about mental health in schools to manage mental illness and break the bias on mental health stigma. In essence Psychologists must be provisioned for in the school system as socialisation is an important aspect in one's life.

Stigma is a social construct element that primarily harbours the self-disclosure of an existing mental illness by an individual with the fear of being labelled or discriminated. However, stigma is an element that can be rectified by the society to vocalize mental health in the society. It is important for one to understand that mental illness, like a headache or blood pressure left untreated, can be a killer; whilst if detected early, treated early, and supported early it can easily be managed through psychotherapy i.e. coping mechanisms and through pharmacology drugs depending on the severity of the condition. Seeking help early is an act of strength and responsibility.

Women are by far the most marginalized and by virtue of their position in society, suffer mostly dire experiences from love and hate, childbearing, post-partum, infertility, violence and abuse, grief and many other physical health challenges such as endometriosis. These dire experiences make them susceptible to mental illnesses including depression, borderline personality, Post Traumatic Stress Disorder etc. Depression if left untreated is like a worm—it eats one slowly from the inside to the point of their death. It can be a lonely road, filled with self-castigation and guilt, described as dying twice as one lives in the moment as if what is being negatively conceived has already happened or is happening, a gloomy and dull road which was once trodden but suddenly has become unfamiliar and unfriendly. Most of the time, ideation of the pangs of death takes over, at times with a plan to either hang oneself, shoot, cut or just sleep it all off... **BEEN DOWN THAT ROAD, SAW IT AND CONQUERED THROUGH IT ALL!!!**

Hope is the only saving grace. Depression feels like the road will never come to an end. One is never in depression, they only go through depression. Reach out and seek help. The beauty of life awaits.

> *The pangs of death surrounded me, and the floods of ungodliness made me afraid. The sorrows of Sheol surrounded me; the snares of death confronted me. In my distress I called upon the Lord and cried out to my God; He heard my voice from His temple and my cry came before him, even to His ears.*
>
> *(Psalms 18:4-6)*

～

Priscilla Sibonginkosi Munemo is a Counselling Psychologist, an endowed Psychologist who has championed empowering women through the re-construction of women's unique lived narratives through Psychology and Counselling. Her work is anchored on the importance of fostering self-esteem, self-efficacy and assertiveness in feminine mental health. Priscilla is also an advocate in the strengthening of women's role in challenging societal inequality.

Having been born in a family of eight in a small mining town of Redcliff, in the Midlands province of Zimbabwe, the vigour to be a woman with a difference is what set the tone for Priscilla. Her first degree in Politics and Public Management from the Midlands State University is what opened her eyes to a world of possibilities through Social Sciences, which after gaining interest in protecting children and women she went on to Women's University in Africa where she completed her Masters in Child Sensitive Social Policies and latter completed a Postgraduate Diploma in Business Psychology from the University of Southwales. Priscilla went on to study an Honours degree in Psychology and latter a Masters degree in Counselling Psychology from Great Zimbabwe University. Priscilla has worked with several organisations. She is now a Counselling Psychologist at Parirenyatwa Mental Hospital.

Knowing and Understanding Your Worth

BY CHIDO MBANGA

I recently listened to a speech, and it was talking about worth and how we get to be deemed worthy or deserving of certain decency, rights, or treatment. Turns out all you have to do is be born and in that moment that you enter the world you are already worthy. You don't have to earn your worth; you just are.

Despite worthiness being readily attainable we still live in a world where we are not all afforded the same liberties. We are still governed by unequal measures and women and girls are on the disadvantaged end of the scale where we are still required to fight tooth and nail to prove that our rights matter, and injustices against us cannot go unpunished, and we deserve equal consideration.

When people are in a position of comfort they are rarely inclined to change the circumstances that they heavily benefit from. The world we live in was not created with women in mind. We were merely objects with no real purpose designed for us and that is shown throughout history, through our laws, through imaginary lines of limits drawn that we were not meant to surpass. The past and at times the present did not account for us to be change makers, to be hungry and to be determined. Instead, we were expected to be content, and our dreams limited.

It is sometimes difficult to see yourself in places that were not designed to accommodate you and that in itself can keep your from reimagining a reality where that's different. It keeps you stagnant, silent, and trapped. Despite the multitude of reasons we as women and girls were not meant to thrive, we continue to exceed all the limitations placed on us.

There is strength and power in consistency. The fight for the girl child is a very long one. In certain times when strides are made, something happens that feels like a step back and to those fighting it can be discouraging. However, it is in those times where we should remain resilient and determined to fight for ourselves because if we won't, no one will. A false narrative was created that dismissed our value and our reason. We were set to remain boxed up and ideas of shattering the glass ceiling were dangerous and meant to be contained. That was an unfounded lie and a fear tactic set up to keep us in line. Our voices, our rights and our thoughts matter and we are not an afterthought.

There is still a gap in rights for women and girls and this brings up the question of whether enough is being done to correct this inequality. The changes made in correlation to the level of significance does not always align and the actions taken do not always make the substantial dent required to close the gap or reduce discrimination in an adequate way.

Research shows that the girl child is still cripplingly excluded and continues to face discrimination at appalling levels at various stages of their lives starting from their early childhood years and this is all on the basis of them being female. The myriad of disadvantages and violations faced by the girl child are not highlighted enough, they are not fully reflected, and they are not made a priority. More progress needs to be made, more awareness on the subject is required, and more education and more tools to equip the girl child to be able to sustainably stand on her own are required. The fight for women and girls rights should be everyone's fight.

Many a time when we take a moment to take stock and acknowledge all that has been done thus far, we get alarmingly shocked by the lack of extensive changes, but this is not to say we stop trying to break the barriers. It just further highlights how deeply entrenched structural divide is and how our systems are constantly failing us, and sufficient work is not being done to fix it. This is a matter of urgency and requires an approach that is active to rightly diminish this unequal gap.

It is unfortunate that in some places, steps are being taken that are setting women backwards. However, our boldness and bravery will not deter us from carrying on the fight. Everything that has happened throughout history, all the ideas, dreams and aspirations created and fulfilled, may we carry it forward with us and let it fuel us to do what needs to be done to move the needle to make it better, not only for the future but for the present.

We may not all live to see our goals materialized but every step each one of us takes individually is vital for all the aspirations put on hold, dismissed, denied, suppressed or still yet to be conjured. Each one of us is important to ensure our dreams flourish and progress. Those of us afforded more privilege than others should be willing to fight harder for those least privileged, especially for things that do not directly affect us. May our actions speak louder than our intentions and instil the same fire and desire in others to want to continue our legacy of change.

I come from a place that often creates the perfect oxymoron, an imperfect balance of contradiction. My home is where the core of my vision and ambition was born, nurtured and in some instances hindered. It's an environment where at times I have felt inhibited but am also being challenged to dream beyond the little that feels possible.

I have looked back and realized I was discriminated against because of who I am, the colour of skin, the size of my body. I was once told my hair takes away from my beauty, presenting myself as less me, that having fewer opinions and less individual thoughts would make me more desirable. In all those experiences and words that never left me I grew more into myself, quickly learnt desirable was not something I was seeking for, I already was, and I had a deep hunger to make an impact. Everything else was background noise and being sturdy in myself would help me attain my ambitions. I have always believed that when we are younger we are more ambitious.

We have not allowed the crippling fear and possibility of failure to constantly have us seconding guessing ourselves and being afraid to take the leap. When we are young there is a certain liberty that allows us to dream beyond our wildest dreams with no barriers, no caps, no obstacles, and no setbacks. It's an open plain field between you and your imagination. That freedom is unmatched adopting that creates an environment where we are unafraid to make big choices about the incredible changes we want to make.

I come from a long line of exceptional women—each one a pioneer and change-maker in their own right. They did not let their struggles hold them back from achieving greatness. They understood it was a collection of both the bad and the good that developed them into the dynamic individuals that they are. I Intend to be just as capable in my own right.

We will often be told what we can and cannot do but it is not for anyone to limit our capabilities and potential. You are boxed and labeled and required to be less to be accepted, to fit a space, where others create and build a space where people like me fit and are considered. I intend to raise my voice and make an impact, be a change maker and do everything in my power to do better. As cliché as it sounds, I want to leave the world better than I found it even if it is just for a singular person.

I never set out to change the world. Believing that only one person's singular beliefs are the right idea of what the world looks like and should shape its existence is essentially why so many people face discrimination every day. I do, however, hope that my constant growth, development and individual evolution and desire to see better for myself does not infringe on anyone else's rights. What I stand for, what I believe and my contributions to the world through my actions promote change for those seeking it and those who cannot fathom a reality where another life, a better life is possible.

Life has an end date. It does not go on forever and between everything we deal with just to catch a breath, it is important that we do something meaningful with what we have. We live in a world that created a space where some people are seen to be less valuable, where some lives do not matter, and when we positively create or are given the ability to do more, we must make the most of that opportunity and not perpetuate cycles of oppression. Our ideas, actions, visions can be revolutionary and that in itself is special. May we not let our biases, both conscious and unconscious, blind us.

Bear in mind what we are actively trying to achieve is a journey, one that is continuous, with different people forging on. It is a journey that never ends, learning and gaining more knowledge grows, evolves, and challenges what we are trying to do and breathes life into more ideas.

Still trying to get it right. Keep dreaming and make your inside thoughts outside actions.

For all those on a mission, sometimes from your view it looks as though you are doing a lot of work but the results don't fell tangible and it makes you want to stop, just take a breath, a moment and keep going. A lot more than you think is happening.

Do not be rigid in your timelines; sometimes you have to account for deference or delay, that does not mean denied. Allow for flexibility, adjustments, course corrections and failures. It's what you do after you fail that determines how far you get. You are never too old or too young to start and you only run out of time when you stop trying.

Chido Angeline Vongaishe Mbanga, is a multifaceted young woman of many talents—some yet to be discovered—and she does not limit herself to any one label. She grows more into herself every day. She is a writer, a lover of learning, and is hoping one day to take part in changing the global economy given her background in Economics and Finance.

Chido is an advocate for all women and girls and wishes to move the needle of equity and inclusion and make sure our voices are heard and we are not disregarded. As an advocate for inclusivity and empowerment, she laces her personal experiences and academic insights into a compelling narrative that challenges societal norms and fosters positive change. She is also just a woman who sometimes watches too much TV and reads a lot. She hopes to do more to be the change she wants to see in the world, love herself explicitly, and continuously seek to be completely herself.

Becoming a Virtuous Woman

AND A FINANCIAL EXPERT
BY ADELINE IJANG

In the pursuit of personal growth and empowerment, women often find themselves navigating a complex landscape that demands both virtuous character and financial expertise. Let's explore how cultivating virtue can enhance financial success, and how financial wisdom can support virtuous living.

I was raised by a community in a typical village setting with the majority of the population being women and widows especially. I never forget where I come from, and the invisible hand of God that has guided me even in my ignorance. As a young girl growing up in a village where everyone is family and every woman is a mother, I learnt early enough that our strength was always drawn from unity not wealth. If you grow up in a culture that practices polygamy, it is possible that if one man dies, two to five women become widows.

My grandfather was a polygamist with four wives, and so when he died, four women automatically became widows. They were all house-wives who depended on their husband and their farms for survival. Ours was not the only family having many widows. Somehow, by the grace of God, these widows managed to survive from their farms and small trades. They were also able to make sure that their children received an education, so as to do better than they did. The amazing thing is that many of these widows never had any formal education, but they fought hard to chase every child loitering around to go to school.

I was only 19 years old when I lost my dad. My family and I cried for many years thinking dad would come back to us some day. But I soon realized that crying does not solve every problem. As the first child in a family of seven children from my dad's two wives, I had to grow up fast so that I could look after my siblings. As if the affliction of losing a dad was not enough, my stepmother died six months after my dad died, leaving behind her three young kids. I realized that death was on a rampage in my community and no quantity of tears would stop the stink of death.

I was not the most brilliant student in class but I was determined to achieve great things through learning. My dad was a school teacher and he died at the age of 46 years, but there was a postcard he gave me when I failed my exam to go to high school. In his postcard to me, he wrote: "My daughter; you will achieve great things through learning, keep learning, I love you." These words were potent enough to push me to where I am today. I kept his words in my heart and I do not intend to forget them. Most parents will encourage their children only when they do well, but my dad was that father who encouraged me when I failed. There is power in spoken words; be careful what you say to your children. We have made monsters out of our children through our words.

Somehow, I had picked up this culture of celebrating every birthday with my friends and family until my thirtieth birthday when I made a switch to practice true religion (taking care of widows). I was reading my Bible a few months before my thirtieth birthday, and a scripture came alive to me. James 1:27 (NKJV): "Pure and undefiled religion before God and the Father is this: to visit orphans and widows in their trouble, and to keep oneself unspotted from the world." I decided to cancel my thirtieth birthday party and redirect all the resources to widows and orphans. I hosted the widows on my birthday and gave them gifts. They had never seen this before and could not believe that a young woman who was not married would gather widows to bless them. They cried, they sang praises to God, they danced, and they prayed for me. From that day on, God placed the burden on me to look after widows. A vision was born.

I believe God answers the prayer of a widow expressly. It is my belief that the prayers of these widows opened doors for me. That same year I moved to Denmark in Europe to for further studies and then immigrated to Canada. It took me twelve years of working with a financial institution in Canada to realize that what God has called me to do wasn't going to work with a nine-to-five job. I needed to find a business that accommodated the vision God gave me, produces results, and changes lives. I chose the financial sector and got licensed as a broker. Today when you ask me what I do for a living, my answer is, "I sell spiritual and financial peace of mind for free." I teach people how to take the little money they have and buy more money. I help families to leave an inheritance for their children's children as the Bible says in Proverbs 13:22. When you're a victim of financial blunder and have learnt through experience, you will gladly give back to families by giving them financial wisdom. That's how you save a generation and leave a legacy. I would listen more to you if you show me your battle scars and also tell me how you overcame. It's hard to take people where you've not been.

In the journey towards becoming a virtuous woman, the foundation lies in the development of key character traits. Integrity, resilience, empathy, and humility are among the virtues that form the bedrock of personal growth and ethical decision-making. Through meditation and intentional practice, women can cultivate these virtues, nurturing a sense of purpose and authenticity in their lives.

While virtues provide the moral compass for ethical decision-making, financial wisdom empowers people to navigate the practical realities of managing money, building wealth, and achieving financial independence. From budgeting and investing to entrepreneurship and career advancement, mastering financial skills equips us with the tools to create a secure and prosperous future. I am out to demystify the world of investing and highlight its potential for long-term wealth accumulation. I am equally out to empower women to assertively communicate their value and leverage their skills for professional growth.

When we aspire to become virtuous individuals and financial experts, we embark on a transformative journey of self-discovery and empowerment. By integrating the principles of virtue with the practical knowledge of financial acumen, we not only achieve success in our careers and finances but also make a positive impact in our communities and beyond. In embracing this holistic approach to personal growth, women empower themselves to lead fulfilling lives guided by integrity, resilience, empathy, and humility, while also securing their financial well-being for the future.

Adeline Ijang (aka: HEAD-GIRL) is the vision-bearer of the Canada Virtuous Women (CVW) organization. She is a financial broker by career and a virtuous woman on an assignment to drive women from their comfort zone to the realm of impossibilities using Biblical principles. She is on a mission to support young widows and their children to become what God created them to be. She is a sold-out believer in Jesus Christ, and an ordained minister of the gospel. She is also an event planner, an international speaker at conferences and a philanthropist.

Adeline holds a MSc in Technological and Socio-Economic Planning and lives in Ottawa, Canada with her family. www.canadavirtuous-women.com

Disability is Not Inability

IF YOU CAN DREAM IT YOU CAN DO IT

BY LILIAN DINO EYONG

"I can do ALL things through Christ that strengthens me," Philippians 4:13.

I was born without any atom of disability in me. I can still vividly remember how I used to run around and play with my elder sister. Being the last child of the family, I was pampered beyond imagination though my family was poor. The love and care I received was unimaginable. I used to pluck garden eggs from my mother's garden beside the house and give it to my elder brother. When Mom saw me plucking even the very little ones, she came after me and I would run as fast as my little legs could take me. It was all fun until that fateful day.

I had a fever and Mom rushed me to the hospital. I got an injection and fell asleep immediately afterwards. Mom brought me home and laid me on the bed. I slept for an unusual number of hours. The next morning, everyone was up doing their chores except me. Mom thought this was abnormal as I was always the first person to wake up in the morning.

She sent my elder brother to check on me. When he came inside the room, I was already awake and sitting on the bed but there was no means to get down from the bed. He told my Mom I was awake already, so she came to find out what was keeping me in the room.

She held my hands and put me on my feet to stand, but I couldn't. She was shocked at first and tried again. I couldn't stand because my legs were very weak. She screamed at the top of her voice. Then, using hot a loin cloth, she carried me on her back and ran to the hospital. Upon reaching there, the doctor told her I was affected by polio and there was nothing he could do about it. My Mom cried and begged him to help me walk again but I guess that was water being poured on a stone.

At home, my dad returned from work and received the shocking news. He was calm and told my mom, "Don't worry too much. Dibo will walk again." That didn't sit well with my Mom as she tried everything that was recommended by neighbors and strangers alike.

One day, she took me to a herbalist that was recommended by a neighbor and my feet were burnt with red hot charcoal. This was the last stroke that breaks the camel's back as my grandma visited during that period and blamed my Mom for putting me through such excruciating pains.

Mom resorted to giving me massages on my legs every morning and night. She would do this while crying and I would cry with her.

One morning while she was giving me my routine massage, a neighbor visited and told my mom, "From the look of things, Dibo is not a normal child. She is possessed. Take her to the river bank at 12 midnight and leave her there. If she is possessed, she will transform into a python and disappear into the water. If she is a normal child you will still find her there in the morning." Upon hearing this, my mom became furious and sent the woman out of our house, telling her never to come to our house anymore.

My siblings loved me all the more as they took turns carrying me on their backs to school and back. My eldest brother insisted that I must go to school like every other child.

In school, I was always the top of the class in primary and secondary level. I passed through all of these with flying colors and was admitted into the university. While at the university, I saw the reality of life—discrimination and exclusion.

I couldn't attend some lectures due to inaccessibility of the halls. At some point, I would sit outside and cry my eyes out. It was traumatizing and I was gradually falling into depression.

Unfortunately, during my second year, the Anglophone crisis broke out and I had to drop out of university. I went home to meet my mom and felt like I was a failure without any skill or a degree.

After two years of sitting at home doing nothing, living a purposeless life, depression finally set in and I started having suicidal thoughts. I couldn't execute this suicidal act because I was always with people at home.

Fortunately, I met a psychosocial counselor and he brought me out of that bondage after a series of counseling sessions and prayers.

Early that year (2019), My elder sister enrolled me in a professional counseling school. During graduation, I was Best Outstanding in Trauma Counseling.

With this encouragement, I decided to inspire other persons with disabilities out there. I started a radio program titled, "Living With Disability."

In June, I heard about the Miss Wheelchair Cameroon beauty pageant and I got registered so as to try my luck. In December 2019, I emerged as 1st Runner Up Miss Wheelchair Cameroon. In March 2020, I launched the Lilian Dibo Foundation for women and girls with disabilities.

I moved from one town to another having radio and television programs advocating for the rights of women and girls with disabilities.

My organization has carried out numerous projects for women and girls with disabilities ranging from education, gender-based violence, sexual and reproductive health rights, business start-up, free arts and craft training, and many more.

As a result of these, I was privileged to win numerous awards as an individual and my organization has two awards for the impact we have created in Cameroon.

In 2022, I was selected to represent Cameroon in Miss Wheelchair World that took place in Mexico.

After the event, I came back home and my organization won three projects which were well-implemented with outstanding outcomes.

Yes! I can do ALL things through Christ that strengthens me. It is evident. Ever since I discovered my purpose, I have never once felt limited. My abilities have inspired so many people both disabled and non-disabled. I am still on the journey of inspiring and motivating people because I want to be the change I wish to see in the lives of these women and girls with disabilities.

I am now a confidence coach as I strive to see more women and girls with disabilities breaking the shackles of disability and exploring the world while living a purposeful life. I want to see them doing and achieving even greater things than I have, to let the world know that disability is not inability and if you can dream it, you can achieve it. I can do ALL things through Christ that strengthens me.

~

Lilian Dibo Eyong is a polio survivor and a wheelchair user. She is Miss Wheelchair Cameroon 2019 and Miss Wheelchair Cameroon World 2022. She has a diploma in Trauma Counseling and is the founder of Lilian Dibo Foundation for women and girls with disabilities. She is the Country Coordinator for Project Peace Lights and a member of the Emerging Leaders Council at Every Woman Treaty, a member of World Pulse and a Confidence Coach.

She has the following awards: Best Storyteller, Inspiring Award, Most Dynamic Leader with Disability, Most Consistent CEO with Disability, Most Consistent Disability Rights Advocate, and Best Outstanding Youth with Disability.

Let's Do More For Girls

THE HOPE OF THE WORLD
BY CAROLYN SEAMAN

Growing up in northern Nigeria, I was at the intersection between my junior secondary school and senior secondary school, at the age of 14 years old, when I was hurled into a reality that I could not conceive for any girl. I experienced the situation where my schoolmate never showed up to school again. When I inquired why she never resumed senior secondary school, I learned that she had been married to her father's friend as a third wife. I never saw my friend again. To this day, I wonder if she ever got the chance to go to school again or complete her education. I wonder if she was quickly thrown into the life of early pregnancies and childbirths and how that took a toll on her if it was the case. I wonder if she ever experienced falling in love and what that was like for her. I wonder if she ever found her voice, considering the fact that she was thrown into a marriage to an elderly man and was surrounded by older wives who were older than her and probably maltreated her. I wonder if the marriage even survived.

If it didn't, I wonder if she was able to build her life again. I can go on and on in my wonders, but I can only wish that she had the opportunity to live even if it was stifled by her experiences. Interestingly, some will argue with my silent wonders and query that I never wondered if she turned out great and her marriage was great, especially if she didn't mind being married at 14. But I beg to differ as I am unsure that any girl would ultimately want to be married at the age of 14. I wish this was just one occurrence in my life, but it turns out to be the story of so many girls across my country, Nigeria, and around the world.

In Nigeria, 44% of girls are married before their 18th birthday and 18% before they turn 15. And globally, an estimated 12 million girls are married before the age of 18. That means 23 girls are married every minute or 1 girl every 3 seconds.[1] Such statistics should make the world rethink the inhumanity that is meted out to these young girls every day, everywhere around the world. But the world is yet to acknowledge it as a form of violence against girls who deserve to get an education and live out their childhood before deciding to be married when they so choose and to whomever they so choose. Sadly, we are not yet close to the indices that will give us the sense that we will see a decline in child marriages or the other challenges that accompany the practice or other forms of violence against girls and women in society. Data reveals that more than 650 million women already suffer the direct consequences of child marriage. And we must face an even scarier statistic that an estimated 150 million more girls will be married as children by 2030 if we carry on like we are today.

In an unfair world where culture and systems are patriarchal, girls and women must live and survive. In a world where EVERYTHING is stacked up against the female gender, girls and women must fight to thrive and fight to make their voices count. How long can we stay silent? How long can we continue to listen to stories that tell us we can lead, or we can be anything we want to be? We must rise above the stereotypes that work to keep us under! We must rise above the violence that beats us down and keeps us traumatized and broken! If we want to truly lead or be anything we want to be, we must RISE above every barrier that tries to limit us.

Those barriers that exist in our cultures and the corresponding social norms that predict that girls don't have to go to school since they will end up in the kitchen anyway, or that women should not work so they don't compete for the headship of the home with the man, or that there are specific jobs that women may do, such as teaching, secretary, or at best nursing, but not as medical doctors or architects or pilots and other such careers. Girls and women CAN DO anything, if only they acquire the skills needed. This is why we demand that girls have equal access to education and opportunities to build the skills they need for their chosen careers.

Hope! That is the hope that I have for a better world for girls and women around the world. Hope that girls can go to school, stay in school, and complete their education as desired. I believe that girls can do and be anything that they want to be. However, we must deliberately invest in the education and empowerment of adolescent girls. It is popularly said that "You train a girl, you train a nation." Once you teach a girl or a woman something, she passes it down to as many as she can around her. And you don't need to make the demand; it is like a natural inkling in her that seeks to share knowledge and experience with those around her. This may be a natural action, but it is common practice that something in her is passed to someone around her. So, why would we fail to invest in our girls? Invest in their education? Invest in her skills building and empower her to explore her potential to its fullest.

Today, we live in a digital world, and we must double efforts to build the capacity of our girls and women to not only survive in this world but to be actively engaged in contributing to society and global advancement. Adolescent girls and women MUST be given the skills they require to take their place in this digital landscape. This changes the game for girls and women. I have seen girls transformed from novices to experts, from shy girls to advocacy champions and fiery activists. I have watched adolescent girls lead a digital campaign on radio reaching over 100 million people around the world with their advocacy campaign from a small radio station in their community. I have watched girls translate from complete novices in the film industry to become award-winning filmmakers using the power of their stories to challenge stereotypes and social norms that limit girls and women. I have seen girls who had no digital skills translate into coders designing websites, mobile apps and even building prototype chips to explore technology solutions to crimes that affect girls like trafficking, and rape. I can go on and on, but the fundamental point here is that girls can achieve mind-blowing potentials if only they are targeted with quality education and contemporary skill building. It is these pockets of interventions around the world that give hope, but we must do much more to move from hope to the reality of a better world for girls and women, a world free of violence, a world free of marginalization, and a world that empowers all – girls, boys, women, and men to live their fullest potential and thrive together in the exploration of their fullest potential. Let's do more! Let's do more for girls and women around the world! Yes! We CAN! TOGETHER, we CAN!

Carolyn Seaman is a lawyer with over 20 years' experience advancing girls' and women's rights. She is a Social Entrepreneur, Tech Evangelist, Filmmaker, Girl Expert, Founder and Creative Director of Girls Voices Initiative, a non-profit that educates and empowers girls and women to identify their voices to advocate for their rights; and to use technology and digital media to amplify their voices to wide audiences, particularly policymakers. Carolyn is a TechWomen Fellow, Women Leader of the World Fellow, World Pulse Ambassador and Advanced Digital Changemaker. Carolyn was named on the 2021 FemiList 100 women, 100 Most Influential Civil Society Leaders in Nigeria, 107 Gender Justice Advocates, Top 21 Women Leaders to Watch in 2021, Humanitarian Awards Global's Most Distinguished Women Change Maker in Africa 2020-2021, Nigeria's 20 Most Innovative Women in Tech, 50 Most Outstanding Female Pacesetters in Africa, Nigeria's 100 Women in Tech and 5 Most Innovative Women in Tech in Nigeria.

A Broadcaster's Route to Confidence

BY RUMBIE CHAKANZA

My name is Rumbidzai which means praise God. I was born the only girl among seven brothers and that challenged me to be brave, strong, and aggressive. I learnt to embrace moments of loneliness, for I had no sister whom I could play with at home. I made the mirror my sister and best friend. On the mirror, I acted like I was addressing audiences, doing public speaking for an invisible audience. I pictured myself as a Radio and TV personality one day. My childhood was filled with so much fun, but also had moments that threatened to kill my self-confidence.

In our society, you are looked down upon for different religious beliefs, especially when you belong to indigenous religions. When going to worship, I would wear my white holy amour and if I met colleagues, some would change paths or ignore when I greeted them, because they didn't want their peers seeing they associated with a person like me. I was laughed at whenever I mentioned my religion Guta Ra Mwari in class. Did that stop me from following my dreams? No! I never gave in to peer pressure my university days; I did not engage in the youthful vices of indulging in alcohol and premarital sexual activities. Religion played a vital role instilling values in me. I had a voice—I could speak up and No meant No. I chose to value a righteous way of living for I believed "A pure soul, a healthy body lives longer in life." This belief inspires me to stand tall and change the narrative.

Furthermore, my motivation to embrace self-confidence is also influenced by an emotional and sad background, where my parents were deprived of the right to education, due to reasons beyond their control. My father was born in a polygamous family in Malawi and his side of the family was given low priority in the family hierarchy. He had to herd cattle most of the time while others attended school. Similarly, my mother with Mozambican origins was asked to drop out of school prematurely by her father and take care of her ill mother.

My parents always portrayed wisdom and intelligence and anyone who had a chat with them would think they had the education and qualifications provided by degrees. They were confident tailors and entrepreneurs and managed to sustain their grocery business until each of the eight of us children finished school in a place they called foreign land. They never let their background deprive us of the right to education. Given their concerted efforts to ensure that my siblings and I received the best education possible, this background gives me the resolve to break the tendency to not value education among marginalized or underprivileged societies.

Due to my academic capabilities, I attended one of the top five high schools in the country, Kriste Mambo Girls High, where I was a Vice Head girl. I was too noisy and got punished always and no one believed I deserved to lead because of that. I did not want the responsibility but the headmaster refused to demote me. I was not confident yet to lead. It's only when I made presentations while doing my first degree, that I realized my voice was powerful. Lecturers would say, "You are a guru in the making, a public speaker." I realized my voice was my strength. I was afraid to participate in public speaking in high school, thinking it was for those who attended group A primary schools, in the low-density suburbs. My high school had girls whose parents were high officials and successful business people and I never thought there was room for me to shine in that field. Instead I was extraordinary in sport and was also the school sports captain.

I started being profiled in newspapers when I discovered my talent as a musician. They say dreams come true. I spent years trying many jobs, while always being drawn to the world of broadcasting, captivated by the power of words to ignite change and inspire minds. I started broadcasting online from home during the Covid 19 pandemic using basic gadgets. I longed and yearned for an opportunity to be a national broadcaster. I spent a whole year of applying and being told there were no vacancies at the time.

One sunny day, I received a life-changing call from the corporation. I had to report for an audition as a radio presenter and producer. I just said "Yes!!!" The lifetime theory I had practiced since childhood developed into reality. I became a radio producer and presenter. It was all natural as I took to the microphone like duck to water. To bolster my confidence further, I sought out mentors who believed in my potential, soaking up their wisdom like a sponge as I gained soft skills that turn talking into broadcasting.

But the road to confidence is not without its obstacles. I endured long hours and sleepless nights, pushing myself to prove my worth in a world that often overlooks women in broadcasting. Some thought I got a "carpet opportunity" or "carpet interview"_euphemism for having sex in the office to gain favours, simply because of my dogged determination of wanting to be the best version of me behind the mic.

I rose fast from grinding on the graveyard shifts to being charged with the responsibility of daytime drive show during peak hours within months of starting on this national radio station. Captains of industries noticed me and my talent and additional roles streamed my way as I became a victor of voices: as a voice-over artist doing TV adverts for government ministries.

And then one fateful day, I was given the opportunity of a lifetime: to direct the ceremony for the corporation's annual musical awards without having prepared for it—just 5 minutes before it started. (My esteemed mentors had instilled in me that a broadcaster's voice is on standby at all times). As I walked to the stage, I started to feel the weight of the task ahead of me. It was enormous, challenging. Yet, I savoured it and embraced it. I felt a sense of achievement and recognition and I never doubted that I could put on a good show. I grabbed the mic with golden hands and shared my golden voice. After the event, more doors opened. It's never about competition for me, but it's all about completion and accomplishment. Never give up on your dreams. Ignore the negative voices on your way up the ladder and work hard and prepare, so you are ready for the "golden" opportunity.

∽

Rumbidzai Chakanza-Mamvura is a broadcast journalist/digital media executive producer, and communications strategist at a master's degree level, with degrees in faculty of communication and information science and commerce.

Rumbidzai aspires to be a Ph.D. holder to offer well researched solutions in communication and media. Outside of broadcasting, she is a singer, as well as a director of ceremonies. She also does philanthropy work educating and uplifting the girl child through her RC Educate Her Foundation. Her goal is to build better communities offering sustainable solutions to change social behaviours.

From Hope to Knowing

A JOURNEY OF HEALING
BY DEBRA MARTINA

W hen you know you know. This is the time we are in right now. The question is: what is it we really know and is it true to our soul? Having turned 60 I reviewed the blessings of my life. I hoped that this would be of benefit to someone, just one person in my life, so that it would mean I had made a difference whilst I was here on earth.

I was a police officer in a rough time but am glad not to be in the force at this time of life and transition. What I decided back then was to be a 'last straw' in people's lives and I know I have been for many. You see, in my police era I saw and attended way too many suicides_where the hope left someone's life and was not able to turn into faith and a knowing that life was good and worth every moment. We would need to find the last person someone spoke to, not to leave the blame at their doorstep but to see what the point of no return was. Then we could close the case. I wanted to ensure that no matter what, if I was the last straw in a person's life it was for them to live and find a higher perspective to go on.

The years of late and where one lives have taken a toll on so many and if you look at most places you may see no Hope. But let me tell you that it is all in the way you look. Our eyes deceive us often, but our hearts when you get to know never will. So, what is HOPE? It is a belief that something may happen to change what we are going through for the better.

We can in despair see the lowest expression of life, and I know that this world places both on display but more often behind closed doors that are the darkest of the dark. Those that come out of those worlds have found the Faith to see greatness of the path but grasp the knowing that they will survive. What I know is that we are now in a time that we not only bring Hope into your life, but will also allow you to survive.

We come to this world not for the experiences we are receiving but for the joy of expressing our true selves despite them. Hope may be what others can help you with, but the real beauty of Hope is when you turn that into Faith. No matter where you find the joy of communion with others the faith still must come from within. It is your connection to the spirit that you are and the Source/God as your creator.

The faith in oneself does not diminish the connection to God but it does redefine many lives. You do not need to worship at the external 'churches' of the world nor is it to worship the self as a temple of itself but as a creator being in the world to be the expression of Source/God. There is nothing that cannot be done when in alignment with the higher power and higher perspectives of our life.

Faith in oneself does not make us the kings or queens over others or special above those around you but it does empower you to be the Unique expression you were born to be. We are not victims of this world. Though stuff happens to us, Source has them happen for us. Hope you can see that we as creators of the world have created the perfect world for us to shine. The darker the world has become the greater the light must be our expression.

I know some are in the frequency of Hope. We can ignite a flame and help protect that light, to fan that to be able to burn on its own. If you can gift that Hope to another at the time when the last straw is about to be expended, you can gift some time. We must use that time to ensure that Hope does not dissipate but blossom into Faith. To see a person as a victim and not able to change their world (including the way we look at ourselves—and often tell our story of victimhood repeatedly) is the greatest disservice we can give to one another.

My journey through seeing the darknesses of the world and working to rid that from the earth has given my heart such joy in seeing the truth of who we truly are. I do not see victims. I no longer fall into the emotions and pains of those still trying to find the hope to survive. Instead, I have faith and know that their soul has the greatest gifts awaiting them and reach out a hand to lift them up any way I can in that moment. This earth is in a new era, and you are the creator of it. Seeing yourself and those around you as the most beautiful, empowered beings (no matter the frequency of their projections in life) will bring you knowing. That is something I am sure of.

Think of a time in your life (which may just be yesterday) in which you were faced with the pains and desperation of living in this dark world. Forces are here to clear this darkness and it has already occurred in my world. I see the beauty of what we have done. Now we can give this vision to those seeking to see.

I can remember pondering the story from the Bible where Christ healed the blind man. As I pondered this as a young child full of questions (who rejected church at the age of 14 yrs.) but never letting go the connection to Source/God, I had a knowing that Christ did not heal him in the way many believe but it was gifting the blind man with the knowing that he was healed and could see. Those around confirmed the miracle. And this is what Hope for Her is to me. Where we find those losing the hope of a better world, hope for some relief from the pains and traumas, we are here not to take that pain and dark world away but to give you a knowing that we are here to help you have faith in yourself as you begin to know 'you got this' because I know you have.

The higher perspective I know that you are is a beautiful, glorious being of God/Source, a powerful creator of this world and all worlds. Where you have hope we are here to help you turn on the faith – not in us but in you. Stop seeing the victims of this world and empower the creators in yourself. No more 'walks of shame' or 'trails of tears' as you are made to leave the structures that have commanded and imprisoned you. Instead, walk on with your head held so high that you command the space to create your new world for you and your loved ones.

Seek out those of this frequency because they are seeking you. Know that you must step forward so that you can be the leader of your tribe into the greater life. You are the greatest light by being you that I will ever meet—just as you are. All you need to do is to step into knowing for yourself of who you truly are.

The knowing stage is sometimes the hardest for us to embrace. The world has such great illusions of the grandeurs of false ideals and idols. I came into this world with a great fear that this time around I would lose myself to this grandeur. However, I know that all that was before me were not failures in achieving but the beauty of the gift to bring the humbleness of myself to the strength of the warrior. That balance is what we seek.

There are times we must stand our ground and make sure that the truth is not corrupted. In that we can create the greatest turbulence in our fields, but this is where your greatest gift will be revealed. Your heart knows what truth is, and you must hold that truth for you and this world. You have a specific piece that is yours to hold and create that no one else can do. You are not in competition with anyone. No one can take what is rightfully yours and you cannot have that of another. So, we must step forward with the knowing that we are here to be supported and to support in a balanced way those that cross our paths. They may be there for a second or they may be there for most of your life, but you are responsible for your part in the interaction. I endeavor to express myself and my truth with kindness and the most empathic tone I can, but many a time I have the voice of thunder from a warrioress and that is okay. I ask that you take the words to your heart to hear and not just the ears where the pain still exists. Take what resonates and leave the rest but the Faith I have in you to hear the words is that you will find the faith in yourself to know you already have it.

Let go the cloaks from others that have shrouded your light. Create the communion for yourself and community in its purest truth. Ignite the Hope of those around you into the Faith that you will do this together in cooperation and non-competition. When you free your light, you can free your family and community and you will be connected to all light in this Universe.

I see you. I believe in you. Go create the world you love for you from the heart with Divine intervention coming not as you see it but at the time God knows you need it, in the abundance that is beyond all the imaginings of your mind.

KNOWING is God inspired FAITH of oneself in the HOPEs of your heart.

Love and starlight, Debra.

~

Debra Martina is a speaker, writer and mentor based in Australia. As a Systems Integrator, she attends to the Collective Consciousness bringing the advent of the New Earth to reality in this Awakening time. She is a Torch bearer for Changemakers clarifying, that if you *'Change your perspective you Change your Reality'*.

She is here to show Restoration is complete and bring that vision to all Humanity where no darkness shall ever exist again.

As you stand in the full light of Source/God you cannot cast a shadow on this world.

Silent Shadows

NAVIGATING CHILDHOOD IN THE WAKE OF
DOMESTIC TURMOIL

BY JEANNIE CUMMINGS

C hildren are often the silent victims in a domestic violence household. When this happens, a veil of secrecy is born. This is where my story begins, in the shadowed corners of a home tainted by turmoil. I wasn't explicitly told to keep quiet, but the weight of embarrassment and shame kept me silent, nonetheless. Who would listen to a mere child? Where could I go, and who would take me in? These questions echoed through my mind, unanswered and unaddressed.

Looking back, it's clear that others knew something was amiss, but most chose to turn a blind eye, pretending not to see the cracks in the facade of normalcy. It was easier to ignore the signs, to dismiss the whispers of distress that lingered in the air like a bitter aftertaste. In those days, it seemed that everyone had their own burdens to bear and delving into someone else's troubles was simply out of the question.

Let's journey back to my early childhood, a time marked by upheaval and uncertainty. My mother left my biological father when I was just four years old, shrouding the circumstances in secrecy. Rumors whispered of gambling debts and broken promises, but the truth remained elusive, tucked away in the recesses of my mother's guarded heart. In those days, questions were left unasked, and the past was a forbidden territory, off-limits to curious minds.

Shortly after my mother's departure, a new figure entered our lives: my stepfather. His arrival signaled a shift in the tides, though at such a tender age, I struggled to comprehend the magnitude of the change. Yet, even in my youthful innocence, I could sense the undercurrents of discontent that pulsed beneath the surface. Unhappiness became my constant companion, its weight pressing down on me like a suffocating blanket, leaving me gasping for air in a world devoid of solace.

Living in a household plagued by domestic violence, I existed in a perpetual state of unease, never knowing what each day would bring. My mother, burdened by the weight of her own pain, turned to me as her confidante, blurring the lines between parent and child in a desperate bid for companionship. With fourteen siblings vying for attention, it fell upon my shoulders to shoulder the role of surrogate, a duty I neither wanted nor understood.

As I grew older, the realization dawned upon me that this was not the life I was meant to live. The constant strain of living in a toxic environment took its toll, manifesting in physical and emotional afflictions that defied diagnosis. Every Friday, like clockwork, a knot would form in the pit of my stomach, signaling the onset of another weekend marred by violence and despair. It was a cycle of anguish from which there seemed to be no escape.

My mother's words, though spoken in anger, left scars that ran deep, fueling a self-loathing that consumed me from within. Her fixation on weight and appearance only served to exacerbate my insecurities, instilling in me a sense of worthlessness that echoed through the corridors of my mind. In her eyes, I was never enough, a constant disappointment that fell short of her unattainable standards.

It wasn't until I found myself working as a crisis counselor in a battered women's shelter that the floodgates of memory were finally opened. The stories of abuse and trauma mirrored my own, stirring echoes of pain that had long lain dormant within me. It was a reckoning that I could no longer ignore, a confrontation with the ghosts of my past that demanded to be heard.

The toll of bearing witness to the suffering of others proved to be too much to bear, triggering a cascade of emotions that threatened to engulf me. The headaches, the fatigue, the overwhelming sense of despair—it was as if my body was finally rebelling against the years of silent suffering, crying out for release from the prison of my own making.

And so, I embarked on a journey of self-discovery, determined to unearth the roots of my pain and reclaim the pieces of myself that had long been buried. Through therapy, education, and introspection, I slowly began to unravel the tangled web of trauma that had ensnared me for so long. It was a process fraught with setbacks and struggles, but with each step forward, I felt myself growing stronger, more resilient in the face of adversity.

Today, as the founder of Uwin Working With Me, I stand as a beacon of hope for those who, like me, have known the sting of abuse and the ache of neglect. My journey from victim to survivor has been a testament to the power of resilience and the healing potential of unconditional love. Though the scars of my past may never fully fade, they serve as a reminder of the strength that lies within each of us, waiting to be unleashed.

As I look back on the chapters of my life, I am filled with gratitude for the journey that has led me to this moment. Though the road has been long and fraught with obstacles, it has ultimately led me to my true calling: to advocate for the voiceless, to empower the powerless, and to ensure that no child suffers in silence ever again. For it is only by shining a light into the darkest corners of our world that we can hope to dispel the shadows of the past and usher in a brighter, more compassionate future.

~

Meet **Jeanice Cummings**, the Relationship Transition Expert. She guides professional single moms to Let go of Past Relationship Trauma to establish boundaries, boost self-worth, and make empowered relationship choices, finding their life partner in Just 6 months. With over 35 years of experience as an international speaker, trainer, and credentialed life coach, Jeanice brings a holistic perspective to her coaching, addressing challenges with worthiness, pride, and self-reliance. As the Founder and CEO of U-Win Working with Me LLC, she utilizes her expertise in psychology, holistic health education, and non-profit leadership to guide women in making better relationship choices and moving forward with courage and confidence. Jeanice's mission is to lead clients from brokenness to wholeness, diversifying techniques to support women's growth and development.

Together We Can

VOICE FOR THE VOICELESS
BY VIOLET OMBAKA

My roots originate from Kenya, Kakamega county, Mumias west sub-County Musanda Emukhwenje village.

Born on 23rd September 1991 (I was nicknamed Mother Teresa) as the last born of the late Henry Wafubwa Ombaka and the late Margret Shiroya Ombaka, I grew up in a family of 12 siblings, 8 surviving (4 boys, 4 girls, 3 whom I never saw). As the last born, I can't say I was handled with a lot of pampering because we were brought up by a mother who was very strong, a disciplinarian, and authoritative but very humanitarian. (I guess those traits helped her not to go through extreme oppression that other women in the village went through at the hands of their husbands and community.) She was nicknamed "Peupe" meaning "Someone who will tell you the truth in black and white, no sugar coating").

My mum was a Jack of all trades—she knew different types of seeds of vegetables that grew well in the rainy and dry seasons, so she used the food at her disposal. Through that strategy, I watched her feed the community during famine periods. I vividly remember her buying food for mentally challenged women and men at our local market in Musanda. My dad on the other hand, whom I lost in 1996 when I was barely 4, (I was told) was a calm, humble, jovial, and very generous man who loved people. He was nicknamed "Akhonya" meaning "Someone who loves helping others generously."

In my community, I grew up seeing people produce sugar cane which used to be sold at Mumias sugar company for processing. Most of the time as a young girl, I could see the majority of those who labored in those sugarcane farms were women. They woke up very early in the morning, as early as 4:00 am to go farming. I saw men waking up late and just loitering around just supervising what their women had done on the farm! After the sugarcane harvesting, the company paid the farmers through men's banks (in which a woman was not a signatory). The person who labored throughout could not receive anything from her sweat. Some women were lucky to receive something after the pay —their husbands bought supper for the family. Others only knew the man was paid when her husband married another woman and brought her home.

Girls were seen as a source of income through dowry even before the age of 18 years. Forced marriage was customary. Women were only seen as objects of sex, giving birth, and taking care of the family. Women were marginalized. They had no voice nor power to own property or the land they worked. Matters of land were only talked about by men and no woman was to be near such talks, as it was a taboo. Their economic, social, and cultural rights were hampered in the name of Culture.They were not even given the family inheritance because they were viewed as objects to be sold to men. This caused them economic hardship and placed them in positions of dependence. The majority of girls remained home and helped with the farm and house chores and did not go to school like boys.

Unlike the other girls my age in my community, I was privileged to be in a family that appreciated both boys and girls and was privileged to be taken to school to attain my primary, secondary, and university education where I studied Communications and Public Relations. When I was in secondary school, I started realizing that women and girls faced many challenges. I became cognizant that women and girls were uniquely vulnerable to certain types of human rights abuses in addition to sexual abuse. Entrenched discrimination against women and girls due to culture in the community had led to various forms of political, social, economic, and cultural oppression and there were very limited avenues for redress. For instance, a defilement case could be handled by area leaders where the perpetrator could bring a cow, goat, or chicken as a way to say sorry for the act and the case could end there, forgetting the wounds it would have inflicted on these poor girls' lives. Sadly, no one cared.

A call for Humanity

My love for volunteering and helping the destitute dates back to my early years. Motivated by a two-year experience working with at-risk women and girls in Kakamega encouraged my desire to serve the community. I volunteered and applied for community volunteering opportunities in different humanitarian organizations. Of course the majority turned me away, but I didn't give up.

In 2012 when I was finishing my diploma and ready to enroll for my degree, a certain organization called the Center for HIV/AIDS Education advertised jobs and I applied for a community mobilizer position. Guess what! I was shortlisted among those who were to go through panel grilling. From the over 200 candidates, I emerged among the top twenty who passed the interview.

The only challenge was that I was placed in Kakamega county for work. Yes it's my home county, but I wanted to enroll part-time to advance towards my degree as I worked. I sat down, pondered about it, and weighed all the options, but the call to serve the community had become very strong. I called one of my elder sisters to ask for advice, and she gave me a simple answer—"Follow your heart!" I finally decided to accept the position no matter what. After all, I could find another university in Kakamega and enroll instead of continuing in Nairobi.

Just like the soul in the Bible, I barely knew this was the beginning of my calling for humanity, a deeper calling to serve. When I arrived in Kakamega to start working with women and girls, trust me I was very nervous and anxious. I was to serve people infected and affected by HIV/AIDS. It was that period when HIV stigmatization was very high in Kakamega county. I didn't have anyone to guide me on where to start. I had never seen or done this before. The Monday morning I was to start work, before I left the house, I went down on my knees and asked God to guide me throughout the journey. It was not an easy journey. I saw women and girls stigmatized and locked in their houses by their family members to hide the shame and people dying due to the scourge of HIV/AIDS.

God answered my prayers and within a month I was on track—you could think I had been doing that work for many years. A few months later I was promoted to field officer and by the time the project was ending in two years, I was the county program manager. When this program ended (earlier than expected), I found it difficult to part with the beneficiaries because of the rapport I had created with them. it took us a lot of effort to bond and reach that point but now it was time to say goodbye. How could I tell them I was leaving for good? It was painful. Our connection and my service to them had ignited my passion, it had fanned my calling into flame. Interacting with them made me understand it's not always that someone needs financial help. Some just want someone to listen to them, to talk to and with them, and help them overcome whatever they are going through.

I left without saying anything to them. They could call me to find out my whereabouts but I kept encouraging them to keep adhering to medication, and promised I would be back soon. Within the seven months I was away, I lost more than 5 women and girls. They lacked someone to motivate them and make them smile. They lost the battle. Their death made me feel guilty for not being there for them. I recall one of them wrote me a letter before her death to let me know how grateful she was for my services, the time I created for them, the awareness I created among people. She urged me not to stay away for good but to remember other beneficiaries who were still fighting but struggling with no one to hold their hands. I thought to myself, what can I do to continue supporting them even without funding. I did not want to ask someone else to help. I personally desired to help and bring about the change I wanted to see.

In 2014 I decided to start a community-based organization called Women Pillar Alliance "WOPA" to support women and girls suffering from injustices, neglect, stigma, and isolation by their own family and friends. I chose to be their voice, friend and hope. I have always experienced a strong communion with the people I serve. Whenever we interact, I feel them calling me for something deeper, a daily reunion with what I love doing. It may be a small community organization but it is driven by a big dream for marginalized people.

I must say, I credit my spirit of service to my late dad. I have also looked up to my late mum whom I lost on 19/12/2021, whom I saw helping destitute people, and my sister Lydia who has dedicated her life to the service of the needy through her sisterhood vacation. I consider kindness as an investment that matures in the times one is most in need.

At WOPA, the main beneficiaries of our work are women, girls, and orphans who are often uniquely vulnerable to certain types of human rights abuses, including physical abuse, sexual abuse, political, social, and economic oppression. For too many of these women, there are very few avenues for redress, especially considering that they live in a patriarchal society where men are the heads of households and women often have little influence in decisions affecting their lives or those of their families. Although each ethnic group in Kenya has its own identity expressed through its cultures and traditions, some deeply entrenched cultural practices threaten the rights of women and girls. Particularly in the Luhya community where WOPA is based, practices such as wife inheritance, paying of a bride price – which creates an idea of "ownership" of the wife by men – and forced marriages are retrogressive and oppressive.

We all in our small ways can be part of the change we crave to see. I believe, If you can cause someone who is troubled to smile, you have done a great thing. If only we can be willing to help each other for the common good, then the world would be a beautiful place for everyone. Mother Teresa said it so well: 'If everyone would sweep their own doorstep, the whole world will be clean." Together we can!

~

Violet Ombaka who is an advocate for social justice, is the Founder and the Executive Director for Women Pillar Alliance "WOPA", a community-based organization in Kakamega county-Kenya. Many call her mother Teresa because of her passion for the vulnerable people in the community. She has over 7 years of experience in project management, working for organizations like Centre for HIV/AIDS Education (CHAE Kenya, Society; held various positions)- as the community mobilizer, Field officer, county manager and Assistant Director. While at CHAE, she was recognized for her positive contribution towards poverty Eradication and stigma reduction among HIV/AIDS affected /infected people in the community. She has served as Programs Manager at Poverty eradication action group (PEAG), CEMAG, Western community empowerment center. A TOT on Control and Management of HIV/AIDS.

She has specialties in Communications and Public Relations, Project management.

What makes Violet outstanding is not only her mastery of project coordination skills but her connection with the beneficiaries as well as turning a worst scenario into a more learning experience.

She's among the 100 Most notable peace icons in Africa, a Sauti Kenya Fellow, Indrani fellow and a board member of various organizations.

The Power of Choice

SOMETIMES IT'S OK TO QUIT
BY CECILIA MZVONDIWA

"Life is a matter of choices, and every choice you make makes you."

-John C. Maxwell-

Ntombizodwa Mzvondiwa, was born in the 70's, at the height of the Liberation struggle, in a small village 65 kms outside of Gweru, a central city in previously known Rhodesia, a former colony of the British Empire and present-day Zimbabwe. This village had only about 300 inhabitants and during the war, was pretty much a rural isolated area with no open hospitals, clinic, and schools. Social gatherings were forbidden, which meant that church services were banned. Rhodesia was mainly a patriarchal society, and their natives knew the importance and supremacy of baby boys. Boys were the ones to carry forward the family name, and they were the ones who could "legally" have the inheritance pass on to them. Her mother Hilda was pregnant for the 6 th time and obviously hoped that this time it would be a baby boy. Much to her parents' disappointment, this time too it was a girl, so they named her "Ntombizodwa," a Ndebele word that literally translates to "girls-only." She struggled with this name for the most part of her early life, not only because it expressed regret for the gender that she was born in, but also for the length. Eleven letters of spelling her name in grade one must have been torture. Her parents were subsistence farmers. Her father lost his job as a receptionist when the English company he worked for closed. Her mother was a stay-at-home mom, and she produced different crafts like woven baskets and mats, as well as molded clay pots to supplement their farming income. Her mother bore two more children, including a boy, after Ntombizodwa, bringing the total siblings to eight.

Ntombizodwa completed her primary school and was then sent to the Catholic Loreto Boarding school. It was evident in school that Ntombizodwa was confident and was born with a strong sense of self. She was ambitious and not shy. She had dreams of becoming a lawyer someday to protect and defend the human rights of those that were vulnerable, especially women. Her only fear was that being strong willed and determined, she might chase her own path in life which may not be aligned with what God wanted for her. It was here at this school that Ntombizodwa first interacted with and subsequently was inspired by the work and lives of the Dominican Sisters, and the Scared Heart Brothers. The Dominican sisters were from Europe, most of them from Germany and had worked and spent a good part of their lives in her country. They worked relentlessly to help the locals do well in their studies. Watching them closely work in the service of others planted a seed in the heart of young Ntombizodwa.

"Even the smallest seeds sown in earnest, when nurtured, become fertile."
- Gene Rumley

She figured if these women could give themselves in the service of locals and were not in any way related to them, she could too. However, there was a challenge in her interest. Her parents were not Catholics, but Methodists. She planned and told herself that she would discuss with her parents during the next school holidays. It was not easy, and she made sure that she broke it down for them into bite-size, easily digestible pieces of information. She received permission to be baptized Catholic and four years later got permission to join the Dominican Sisters when she graduated from high school. She was given a new baptized name Cecilia, which of course was a welcome change.

"Life is about choices. Some we regret, some we're proud of. Some will haunt us forever. The message: we are what we chose to be."

- Graham Brown

Life for Cecilia in the convent was exciting. She was aware that one does not wake up and become a sister, brother, or priest overnight. There is an intensive training period that goes with it. The process she went through with the Dominican sisters started with what they called Postulancy. This is a one-year period where it was like an open invitation to "come and see." So, it was here first, that she learnt the practice of meditation, reading the bible, reading spiritual books, and learning about the stages of personal and vocational development. The process would continue further in stages and were as follows:

- Postulancy - one year "come and see period"

- Candidacy - one year – preparation for novitiate
- Novitiate – two years – this was the intensive formation period, and preparation for first vows.
- Juniorate- 3-5 years – this was discipleship time, where one would deepen their religious journey by getting involved in the missionary work as a teacher, nurse social worker or other areas.
- Final Commitment – this is when one would take the final commitment of the 3 vows of chastity, poverty, and obedience until death.

Cecilia was loved by all during her training period. Her youthfulness and energy attracted many in the convent. She was highly engaged in different programs such as coaching and training the youth, conducting retreats, composing songs, and teaching music. Thinking back, she would later joke about her life in the convent during discussions with people and say, "I was almost a celebrity nun, more like Sister Act." She had a television program called "extra time." This was broadcasted at the end of the day during closing time at midnight on National Television. She would record thought-provoking reflections like a 'thought of the day' and had many followers who looked forward to the times when it was her turn to close the broadcast. She was also invited to radio stations to discuss Christianity, Catholicism, and religious life. Life was going great.

As she progressed with her life as a junior Sister, Cecelia felt this burning passion for doing more and scaling her impact beyond the catholic realm, beyond Zimbabwe. Those were big thoughts, yet scary at the same time. For that to come to fruition she may have to leave the convent and start a different life. It was terrifying for her. Her biggest fear was what would her parents say. What about the many people who watched her on TV, listened to her programs on the radio, and the ones who attended her retreat? Becoming a lawyer was still on her mind.

Cecilia struggled with these thoughts for some time and finally gathered the courage to speak to the mother superior in charge. The response from the mother superior again was very clear that being a lawyer was not an option. However, the mother superior understood her predicament. It was the year that Cecilia and 3 other colleagues were preparing to do their final commitment. She looked forward to going for an 8-day retreat hoping to clear her mind on what she wanted and what God was saying to her. Cecilia was looking for confirmation, in a quiet solitary recluse by listening to the whisper of the Almighty.

"The more decisions that you are forced to make alone, the more you are aware of your freedom to choose." -Thornton Wilder

When the time came, Cecilia travelled to Macheke, 91 kms from Harare to a monastery to spend 8 full days in total isolation and prayer. The retreat was directed by one of the Monks, Rev.Robert Igo. It was not easy. In those 8 days she wrestled almost every night as Jacob in the Old Testament did. This was not just a decision about what house one wants to buy, or the dress one wants to wear. It was a decision about who she was and her true purpose in life. She prayed for courage to overcome the fear, and the possible back lash that would ensue, after making the decision to leave the convent, especially from her family, relatives, and friends. The insight that God gave her was if she was not happy, there was no way she would be a be good servant of God and represent him. She also knew that it would be better to leave the convent before the final commitment rather than later. Cecilia decided to leave the life she had known for nine years.

"Your life changes the moment you make a new, congruent, and committed decision."- Tony Robbins

Having made her decision, it was not easy to communicate it to her director who was in charge of the junior sisters. The first question that she was asked by the director was if she was pregnant. Cecilia answered in the negative. The next question that followed was whether she was in love with a man, to which Cecilia again replied in the negative. She was then asked to give a more concrete reason as to why she had decided to change her mind. She wanted to talk about impact, influence, and her passion to make a difference in the lives of others, to live a purposeful and significant life with intention. To experience freedom in doing what she felt was right, for the greater good of society, beyond Zimbabwe and even to the world. None of these thoughts came out orally during that meeting. Instead, she just mentioned that she wanted to pursue her desire to become a lawyer. She was then asked to give it time and think again. However, Cecilia knew that her mind was already firm and made up.

"Above all be of single aim; have a legitimate and useful purpose and devote yourself unreservedly to it."

– James Allen

She also believed that when it is the right decision, doors open, and one finds confirmation. And it did. It was at this time of struggle that she leaned that her only brother, who was younger than her, had moved to Canada from South Africa in September of 2001. When she shared with him, he suggested she too could move to Canada when she left the convent. At that time, Zimbabwe was a commonwealth country and all one needed was to purchase a ticket. When she went home to tell her parents, they were surprisingly supportive to her. Her father told her that life is about following one's heart and being the person you are called to be.

"You must first be who you really are, then do what you need to do, in order to have what you want."

- Margaret Young

With the blessings of her parents, Cecilia made haste to plan for her departure. She inquired of her brother the city he was in, so she could go to a travel agent and book a ticket. She had no money but believed that she would receive help from friends and raise enough money for the ticket. Her brother was in Montreal. She had never heard of such a place. She had only read about the Canadian Rockies, the "Red Indians" (now the acceptable term is Indigenous people) and Toronto. She was excited and nervous at the same time. She had never left the country before. She had never experienced flying before. She wanted to experience all the freedom she possessed and take responsibility for her life from now on.

Three weeks after Cecilia left the convent, she was on a plane to Canada. She left the convent, the country, and the African continent to go and start a purpose-driven life in a faraway country. It was scary but an adventure too. She initially struggled to integrate into the new country and new lifestyle. Here no one knew of her past and she never spoke about it for the first eight years. It took her that long to be comfortable talking about her experience in the convent and her decision to leave it midway.

She started off in Canada getting requalified in Human Resources, added numerous certifications to her credits, worked as a human resource professional for fourteen years before transitioning into her dream of practicing as a lawyer.

"When you stay on purpose and refuse to be discouraged by fear, you align with the infinite self, in which all possibilities exist."

-Wayne Dyer

She feels grateful for the path that she has travelled thus far and the growth and development that has occurred within her. She believes that someday she will be one of the most influential lawyers because she brings a unique background that most lawyers have not been privileged to have. Among many other achievements today, Cecilia has coached over 3000 leaders in an organization with more than 120,000 employees. She has coached women who are going through separation and divorce as a divorce coach. She has facilitated hundreds of new Canadians' immigration processes from across the globe as an Immigration consultant. She has challenged individuals, municipalities, and organizations to end racism and be more inclusive as a Diversity, Equity, and Inclusion Consultant. She is the first ever Appointed Hate Crimes Liaison for the government of Alberta where she advises the Ministry of Justice and Public Safety on how to prevent hate crimes. She is a sought after Keynote speaker and in 2024 on International Women's day she received a Distinguished woman of Influence Award.

Cecilia is a big believer in the power of the mind and the willpower to be what she wants to be. When she reflects back to what has been her mantra in life, it was that "what you think, you become, what you feel, you attract and what you imagine you create", the power to decide always was within her, to live the life she wanted. Recollecting back to the time and circumstances in which she was born, nothing makes sense when compared to the life that she now lived for the past 10 years. Flying on a plane almost weekly, speaking and attending international conferences, staying in all sorts of hotels, travelling first class and sitting in many executive lounges in Europe, America, Africa and Australia, she often had to pinch herself to believe it was true, having grown up in a village, with mud huts and a humble beginning, to the place she now finds herself in. She was now doing what she loved and doing it with passion, and it all came after a decision she had to struggle with.

The big challenge is to become all that you have the possibility to become. You cannot believe what it does to the human spirit to maximize your human potential and stretch yourself to the limit.

-Jim Rohn

The one trait that has carried Cecilia through is the openness and willingness to learn. She confesses that she is a life-long learner, having learned so much both academically and experientially. She has realized that the more she learns, the more there is to learn. She believes in the infinite potential of what the universe has for her and that she is still moving towards being the best version of who she is supposed to be. When adversities and challenges come, she takes it as an opportunity to learn and grow herself through it. Cecilia is a successful mompreneur who runs two successful businesses and is a woman of influence.

~

Cecilia Mzvondiwa is an author, speaker, and entrepreneur who champions diversity, equity, inclusion, and belonging. As CEO of Global People First, she consults for top organizations like BBC and Wells Fargo. Founder of OnPoint Law, she empowers marginalized communities with access to justice.

Her Hope

HOW MY SOCIALIZATION AFFECTED THE WAY I
LOOKED AT THINGS AS A WOMAN
BY LINDIWE MAKONI

"You should dress like this, eat like this...If you ever want to be married you need to change your attitude...and all other naggings a lot of my African women can relate to. We had a lot of role allocation that felt suffocating since I was a little girl. If I was accused of something I didn't do by an elder, I was taught I should not stand up for myself because that will be disrespectful. So, I learned to swallow my words until I was married. If I go into that then it would be one of the best fiction stories you will ever read. It was not a nice experience at all. I was trying to be a good wife with no mouth. It made me open to abuse and I took, thinking it was normal.

I had low self-esteem. I even believed I was one of the ugliest people and was not sure if I would satisfy any men. So, the little attention (or none at all) was a favor to me. One of my cousins scolded me, asking why I always covered myself up without showing my figure which he said was good. You can imagine how I felt, thinking he was trying to be kind to his sister.

Words don't have a bone or body, but they can be as cruel and damaging as any physical attack. I could not overcome my childhood abuse and the psychological abuse I endured in my marriage, but thank God, I was able to walk out after three years and decided to go back to school. I was labeled the hot head of the family for not dealing with the heat and told I should have suffered quietly and been a good wife. If I had not gotten pregnant first, I might not have been in that situation. However, because we marry for the wrong reasons, we suffer in the process. What pains me more is watching women stay in that bad relationship for societal status and living a miserable life.

I went to college and did my diploma in education, leaving a baby who was eleven months old. I left her with her father. All that is for the next chapter. After walking out of the bad marriage. I started on a journey of finding myself and understanding some puzzles in life. One can be called "loose" or "home breaker" or "evil," not because they are but because everyone happens to have a definition of what they see. I started unlearning most of what I learned from childhood. It was and is hard. Some things were imprinted on our brains and letting go is hard. But some of the things have helped me be in this position today.

- Not worrying about what the next person thinks about you
- Doing things because you want to, not to please other people
- Going for your dreams
- Being your brand without comparing to anyone
- Above all else, loving yourself as you are—I found out the hard way no one can do that for you.

I decided that as an educated woman, I would be able to do most of the things I thought only men could do. I did my first degree in Psychology, which was crazy because my motivation was from an abusive husband who said, "You have a diploma already. Why waste time in getting a degree?" I thank him even now because I had to prove him wrong and went ahead and did it whilst I was breastfeeding my third and last child. The choice of the degree was also to try and find out how men think. Yes, silly me. I am still puzzled and have no clue at all. But I understood one thing—with education you get exposed to better things and can reach your dreams. I had a good job and continued with reading and having more diplomas and degrees. As they say, there is no limit but just your energy to continue.

I had to go through reflection on myself, counseling, and reading to understand how my childhood trauma affected my behavior and everyday life. It was hard to deal with but one thing I can tell you is it's a process.

You have to be patient, take it one day at a time, and keep on loving yourself. Be your own cheerleader and be patient with your beautiful self—Rome was not built in one day. You are unique and beautiful in your own way. Never compare yourself to anyone and remember there is no one competing with you. Do you! It's ok if you fail—you will be better as long as God gives you the present of another twenty-four hours to fix the mistake. Find something to smile about every day, and be happy.

∽

Lindiwe Makoni is an Experienced Educator, Versatile Marketer, and Aspiring Clinical Mental Health Counselor

She is a dedicated and dynamic professional with over 20 years of diverse experience in education, sports administration, and international marketing. She is adept at navigating different cultures and behaviors and committed to promoting equality and understanding in society, fueled by a lifelong passion for unraveling human behaviors. Currently Lindiwe is in the final stages of a Master's in Clinical Mental Health Counseling, leveraging a unique blend of skills to empower individuals on their journey to self-discovery. She has led successful marketing campaigns, adapting strategies to diverse markets, gained invaluable insights into global cultures and consumer behaviors.

Thank You, Mama

BY SEKIMAZ MBANGA

2008

"I hate you so much sometimes. How could you stay with Dad for so long? How could you let him do this to you? To us? Every day, I look at you and I see a weak woman. A woman who stayed with her cheating husband. For what? For money? For security?

Why couldn't you leave him? Why couldn't you say 'Enough is enough'?

You can't support yourself because of the love for that man. I HATE him so much, even as I love him. But most times I hate you more. Why couldn't you be an independent woman able to stand on your own two feet? Why could you not love your children enough to leave him?"

Tariro watched from the doorway as her mother closed her journal and took a deep shuddering breath. Her head remained bowed for a few minutes.

"She must be so angry with me." Tariro thought to herself as she prepared to enter the room. "Well, she can be as angry as she likes. Serves her right for reading my private journal."

As she was about to push the door fully open, she saw her mother wipe her eyes. Tariro paused.

Her mother was crying? Her mother never cried. Even when she found out her husband had been cheating on her she never cried. Not once in her sixteen years had she ever seen her mother cry, except at a funeral. Tariro's anger evaporated, to be replaced by concern for her mother and uncertainty. She hesitated, debating whether to confront her mother or walk away and pretend that she hadn't seen her tears. She must have made a sound for her mother looked up and saw her. For what seemed like a millennium, neither one moved, neither said anything. Her mother took a deep breath.

"Tari, come here, I need to talk to you." Her mother held out her hand and waited for her eldest child to make up her mind. Something in Tariro, some inner voice from a deep rooted, self-preservation instinct screamed at her not to take that hand. That life for her was never going to be the same. That this was the end of her childhood. That she would never be the same again. She took a step back and made eye contact with her mother. What she saw in her mother's hazel eyes stopped her from retreating further. The pain and disappointment she read in those eyes had her taking the first step forward. The love and determination had her taking those final steps.

2020

Tariro stood silently by her mother's grave. The light rain barely registered as she stared at the coffin. She had known this day would come, but that knowledge still could not prepare her for the loss. The void left by her mother's death was so vast, so crushing Tariro found it hard to breathe sometimes. She wondered how she would manage without her mother in her life. A woman she spoke to every day, her confidant, her biggest supporter and greatest critic. She thought back to the day of her sixteenth birthday when she found her mother reading her journal. A day that was irrevocably etched in her mind and heart. The day she found out that not only had her father been cheating on her mother for the entirety of their marriage, but that he had also effectively killed her. He had infected her with HIV.

She wiped her tears and looked up to the sky.

"If only the Lord could tell me why she had to leave now. She barely had enough time to know her grandchildren." She rubbed her protruding belly. "And one grandchild she will never get to know," she thought bitterly. Tariro thought about her six-year-old daughter Tanatswa and three-year-old son Tongani. She wished she could talk to her mother right then, instead of staring at her final resting place. Lord, it was so hard. The only thing that kept her standing was the knowledge that she had to be strong for her children. They were the source of her strength. That and everything her mother had raised her to be. The inner strength and courage passed down from a generation of strong-willed women. Women willing to suffer and endure for their children and families. Crying even harder, Tariro pulled out the letter she had written to her mother and prepared to have their final conversation.

Thank you, Mama. Thank you for loving me enough to punish me for the wrongs I did. Thank you for loving me every moment, especially those times when I thought you didn't. Thank you for the discipline and courage you taught me.

Today I look in the eyes of my daughter and I can see how strong you were. I look at my daughter and I can see how much you sacrificed for us. How much you suffered to ensure that I could grow up to be the person I am today. Looking back, I am so grateful for who you were, for showing me who a mother should be. Although I would not make the same decisions you made, I can understand why you made them. The sheer vastness of the love you had for us, your children, that led you to make those decisions. I can understand how angry you must have felt every time you found out Dad was cheating. How devastated you must have been when you were diagnosed as HIV positive. The shame and stigma you must have felt. As Africans this was something that could not be discussed, a burden you could not even share with your siblings. Through all that, not once did I ever see you let it affect you. You remained strong and steadfast in your love for us, showing us the endless joy of life and family.

I look at my children, especially Tanatswa. My little girl who is so like you it scares me sometimes. My heart feels like it will burst with the love I have for her. Now that I am a mother I know that there is very little that I would not do for my children, nothing that I would not sacrifice for them. I know that you are physically gone but you live on in me, in my siblings and in my children. I hope I can carry on your legacy and the legacy of all the women who stood before you. Women who shaped who we are today and hopefully who we raise our children to be tomorrow. I hope that I will continue to make you proud. That wherever you are you can also be proud of your grandchildren. I love you, Mama.

Tariro kissed the hand-written letter and released it. It seemed to float in slow motion. She watched as it swayed and shimmered until it settled on the wooden casket. With a final goodbye, Tariro turned and walked away.

~

A Bridge to the End

BY UMMI MUSE (19 YEARS) NIGERIA

G ender-Based Violence is a form of violence where one gender abuses the power they have over another gender (in most cases, the female gender). This has been a menace for quite a while and its growing and recurring nature through its old ways and even newer ways is very alarming and demands our collective voices and strongest actions to bring an end to it. It is only through a general mindset programmed to see an end to this menace and our collective strength, determination, and perseverance that we find a guide to walk through the bridge of gender-based violence directly to the end.

In most cases, particularly in Africa, the after-effect of gender-based violence often leaves its survivors to an unjust social system or to frustration, depression, diseases of the heart and body, unplanned pregnancies, unplanned childbirths, forced marriages, low self esteem, inferiority complex, death, or even suicide as the list goes on and the culture of silence has only done more harm to this menace. It is significant to understand the importance of speaking up and breaking the culture of silence by victims, their loved ones, and witnesses.

The most significant path on the bridge to this end is to inhabit the culture of breaking the silence of gender-based violence survivors in every form; sexual, physical, domestic violence, or even emotional and economic abuse. And this does not only relate to the survivor alone, but also related to her closest relatives and the public. It is important that we all join hands in speaking up for the survivor and against the perpetrator while still acting on other roles like being a safe space, abolishing shaming of survivors and archaic cultures that victimize girls and women, encouraging and volunteering in support groups with genuine intentions, educating the men and boys on their role in this to the society, protecting the victims from stigmatization, charging the government and law enforcement agencies for reformation and re-strategizing the justice system on perpetrators and enforcing the laws.

Research shows that a perpetrator, if not punished, has the potential of abusing 400 other girls. The danger of silence is enormous and unrewarding, however, breaking the silence is a way of eating our cake and still having it because by speaking up, we are stopping the impunity that would have continued, we are demanding and getting justice, starting the journey to healing, and also protecting our sisters in the larger society. It definitely is more than just speaking up; indeed, it is gaining victory against the perpetrator/abuser and building the victim to the beautiful and self-fulfilling journey ahead.

Gender-based violence keeps getting closer to everyone as research in Nigeria has quickly moved from 1 in every 5 women to 1 in every 3 women found to have experienced some form of gender-based violence. And this emphasizes an increased need for collective action against gender-based violence because one can never tell when it just might come in our direction. Survivors need to understand that they are never alone and there is always a point to re-start the journey and join the fight to put an end to ALL forms of Gender-Based Violence.

Ummi Musa 22, is an outspoken advocate of the law and is currently engaged in her studies in law. She has also become a successful entrepreneur.

Her yearning for girl child development, enthusiasm in advocacy and social services has driven her to a number of contributions, investing in coaching a number of individuals on the same path, actively volunteering in several development projects and pursuing a series of seminars and conferences to support her in her causes.

Ummi has a brilliant track record in leadership and interpersonal skills as she relentlessly pursues her passion and personal development. She continues to explore the world to contribute to global change.

Breakthrough

BY FAVOUR CHUKWUGOLUM (20 YEARS) NIGERIA

I am drowning in a sea of nothingness.
You are ripe enough for marriage.
Your husband is coming to pick you up.
You are his now and you must take care of what has been given.
Images of my thoughts were flying.
But I didn't see or catch the symbols.

Singular action, series of emotion
It morphs into something different.
Pushed into that wormhole.
Having to be a Paramour
Because I never said yes
There is a stopper forced into my exit.
And never from the claw can I escape.

Be silent, he said.
But even in my silence, it is marked with chaos.
It's quiet but those are my demons.

I can't even hear my own thoughts.
I dance to the tune he plays.
I act to the script he writes.
I adapt to one beat, and he changes the rhythm.
Then I am confused all over again

They made a mess out of me.
Because I didn't turn out to their perfect picture
Then they tried to fix me
They try to paint me to mend me.
And then like tattered rags
They stitch me, trying to fix.
In the process they keep tearing
And cutting and breaking me into tiny little pieces

Because I've grown into a jigsaw puzzle
They tried to play me, to solve me.
We are to be blamed for destroying you at that time, we thought it was
the right thing to do,
they spoke.
They make the mistake, and it swallows me up.
Left unconscious of the effect of their actions.
They fail to realize how much or how little things could change.
Actions speaks louder than words, but words hurt twice as much

Silence is my hate.
So, I broke it.
The quiet is violence.
So, I broke through.
I see lights in this dark room.
So, I reflected it
Then my silence is serenity and my quiet peace

I did all that I did to become me.

Breakthrough girl!

For in you is a fighter that liberates a lot more.

Favour Uzoma Chukwugolum is a passionate girls' rights activist and Chair of the Adolescent Girls Advisory Board at Girls Voices Initiative Nigeria. She supports the organization's mission to create a safe space for girls to share their voices for social change and the protection of girls right.

Favour was selected among Women of the World 40 Young Leaders to mark the International Day of the Girl in 2021, and has held various advisory roles including; Strategic Design Team member and Fund advisory member under With and for Girls Fund, the African Conference on Sexual Health and Rights Youth Steering Committee member, and she is currently a member of the Young Women Institute of the Pan African Alliance to End Child Marriage.

Freedom

BY ESTHER AMASIANYA (19 YEARS) NIGERIA

I was born in uncertainty, shaped in doubt.
I lived in obscurity; I lived in fear.
Sit in silence they said, your words must be measured.
My gender seemed to be the definition of my capa-
     bilities.
I was unplanned, a product of many failed tests.
But one success seemed to be a failure as well.

It's quiet and I can hear my thoughts.
Words flow back and forth.
A stone memory sends spirals down the river of my
     heart as tears leave my eyes to join the flowing
     stream.
The oddity that never fitted in
The red gash on a white canvass
But in my mind, I'm bold and strong.
This chasm I pushed myself into,

This hole I let trap me in,
It's quiet but these are my demons.
Silence is my hate.
This quiet is violence.
So, I part my lips and let the words come.

I refuse to be shut down by the words that undermine
my abilities.
I chose my pain to become my motivation.
I chose to break out of that silence and open the doors to
the chasm of my heart.
Now, I stand before a white canvass, the palette in my
hands and the brush at my fingertips.
The crisscross patterns painted by uncertainty has
become my art.
Because I am what I chose.
And I chose Freedom.

Esther Amasianya, 23, is a driven and passionate advocate for gender equality, dedicated to creating inclusive and impactful initiatives. With a degree in Law and a commitment to personal and professional growth, she places value on excellence, leadership, knowledge, and societal relevance. By seeking to leverage her legal expertise and passion for social justice, Esther strives to drive meaningful change and foster a more equitable society through her initiatives and advocacy work. Esther recently successfully completed a course in AI Career Essentials with ALX Africa and is currently advancing her studies in Emotional Intelligence to enhance her advocacy efforts.

Don't Lose Hope

BY PEACE I. GARBA (18 YEARS) NIGERIA

There are times in life when you are alone
Times may come when there is no one to pick you up and dust you
when you fall,
Sad moments may come when you feel like giving up,
Don't lose hope

Situations may arise when you can't relate your troubled moments to
your parents, friends, and loved ones.
So much bad energy from the people you least expect such from
You bottle up a lot of feelings and burdens that lead to heartache,
Don't lose hope

It becomes clear and obvious to you that you have not only lost your
peace of mind but you are beginning to lose your sanity,
Yes! Your relationships with loved ones and friends get ruined, please,
stay strong.
It's ok to cry but
Don't lose hope

On the road to success, there are always giants.

On the road to success, there is always WE not ME.

There is always someone who is praying for you, ready to hold your hand and walk with you through thick and thin.

There is always that person who will whisper in your ear, "You are not alone!"

In every trial, struggle, and storm, you are not alone!

Don't lose hope; you are not alone!

Peace Iyabo Garba is a dedicated graduate of sociology from the University of Abuja, Nigeria. Her personal experiences and academic journey have fueled her passion for advocating girls' rights and promoting the Sustainable Development Goals (SDGs). With a deep commitment to creating a positive impact, Peace actively engages in initiatives that empower young girls and address issues of gender equality. Her work aligns with global efforts to achieve the SDGs, particularly those focused on education, gender equality, and reducing inequalities. Peace's dedication to her cause is evident in her advocacy efforts and her drive to bring about meaningful change in her community and beyond.

The Power of An Adolescent Girl

BY CHIDO MBANGA

S o many times it is said that she loses control of herself, as the raging hormones of finally becoming an adult precede her, with an impairment of what she is truly becoming, a woman. The woman in her is finally escaping her youthful cocoon. Through this she is fighting the trouble every youthful soul is exposed to but because of her strength she does not succumb to them. Instead, she rises above them all. That is a powerful adolescent girl.

Being an adolescent girl comes with many responsibilities. Everything she ever does is watched closely but because of who she is, she takes accountability for her actions. She is an ultimate warrior. When educated she is not only feared but she is a threat to an extent that not even her mind can fathom. That is a secret most girls are yet to discover. She can do anything she wants as long as she sets her mind to it. The power she possesses is not in being the best but in always doing her best. She strives and thrives for success no matter the obstacles. The girl child is not perfect. She falls often, but what differentiates her from everyone else is she is able to get back up regardless of how hard the fall was. These are the few things that make an adolescent girl powerful and a story worth telling.

However true the strengths she has are, there is a constant battle she faces, which is sticking to who she is. We all have an identity crisis. To win this battle all she needs to remember is that there is no better version of her except her original self. As an adolescent girl she has to be herself all the time. She should not be afraid of standing firm in her beliefs or doing the right thing because it is right. She should not follow the crowd, instead she must be hell bent on starting her own walk. Once she understands that she will richly grow. Being different is not a bad thing. It shows that she has a strong-willed character, and nothing makes her happier than being who she truly wants to be. She strives to not be a people pleaser because no one is ever completely happy. Keeping this as a constant reminder builds a strong foundation of her womanhood. It helps her live up to her true nature of being a powerful girl child.

Until

BY TAMARACK VERRALL

Until girls are not killed at birth for being girls
Until we are welcomed for the gifts that we are
Until every girl goes to school
No more attacks from uncles, brothers, cousins, fathers,
     grandfathers,
Strangers,
No more keeping us indoors.
Until forced marriages end,
No more selling,
No more indentured labor,
No telling us what to wear.
Until there is no more violence, no more beating up, no
     more rape,
Until there is no more acid thrown in faces,
No more honour killing,
No more cutting, no more girls screaming in pain,
Until no more hot rocks are pushed against budding
     breasts,

No more breast ironing
By mothers out of fear for their daughters becoming
    women,
Until we are cherished, respected, safe from the fear
That some man will rape us, will rape her,
Without fear
That I will, that she will, that they will
Disappear tomorrow and be discovered dead in a river,
In a barn, in a brothel somewhere far away from home,
Or in her home.
Until womanhood is held sacred,
And every girl has what she needs when she bleeds,
Until untouchable is a word of the past,
And seclusion is chosen, never forced,
And until old women are free of forced mourning in
    mourning huts,
Until no woman loses her home and land when a
    husband dies,
Until no woman is forced to marry his brother or lead a
    secluded life,
Or a life on the street,
Or pushed into a ditch to die in fire, labelled a witch.
Until women live freely and safely with dignity,
Until there is no more
Ridiculing of young single mothers,
Scathing rebukes for loving without knowledge,
For birthing without health care,
For mothering without community,
Until girls do not disappear into slavery,
Until there is no more pornography,
No more taunting words and grabbing and threats

*For being alone on a walk, for being alone on the way to
   school,*
On the way to work, on the way to friends,
*On the way to meet a lover, on the way to read a book in
   the park,*
On the way to drive a car,
*On the way to do whatever we want with our days, our
   evenings, our nights.*
*Until we have the time and space and liberty to write
   and speak and meet,*
*Until all women speakers and journalists in jails are
   freed,*
Until we are not held captive and tortured
For speaking the same words as these,
Until our words are free and heard.
Until this world built on violence and corruption,
Selfishness and squandering,
Money hoarded offshore is
Brought back to the communities it is stolen from,
Distributed to the people who mined those mines,
The farmers who fed their communities,
To the schools, the hospitals,
Until poverty is ended, medicine available
Until people and animals are not dying from
Chemicals in our water and land,
And endless wars over wealth,
*While we witness the ruination of our magnificent
   Earth.*
*Until the truth of what women have done and do is
   known,*
Until our wisdom and beauty is understood,

Until women emerge from these lives, imprisoned and
    controlled,
This containing of our spirits, the forced silence of our
    graves,
Until every girl grows up strong and free, her opinions
    heard,
Until we have the time and space and liberty to write
    and speak and meet,
Until we form new leadership for this world,
Until the brilliance of our leadership soars,
Our writing of history, the truth of the past,
The truth of now,
The emergence of visionary ideas,
Connected with each other globally,
Celebrating each step forward,
Until every woman lives free
And then, until.

~

Previously published in *WorldPulse*

Hope for Her Global

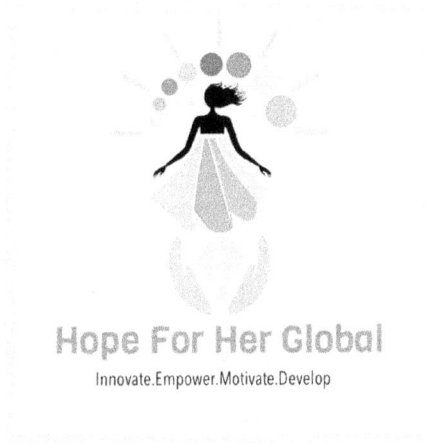

Hope For Her Global
Innovate.Empower.Motivate.Develop

Enhancing Women through Education, Empowerment, Motivation, and Inspiration

The goal of **Hope for Her Global** is to assist women in all aspects of adaptation and integration:

- Work towards improvement of the lives of women and the girl child in local communities Nationally and Internationally.
- Support women, especially local women to acquire skills and access to micro credits that will make them less dependent.
- Provide women from all walks of life with a united voice to speak out on issues affecting their day-to-day lives.

- Empower women, female leadership that will lead common involvement in pressing for a solution to the current crisis.
- Empower women who in turn will empower others by facilitating workshops and virtual webinars.
- We are dedicated to giving young girls and the youth, practical tools and ideas to help them navigate life.

Values and Purpose

We strive to embody the vision and spirit of HOPE FOR HER GLOBAL creating a community that positively impacts our communities, your communities, cities, regions, or countries.

Chapters and their activities are powered by volunteers and must never be driven by personal, religious, or commercial agendas. We focus on generating impact and change in local cities and regions.

GIVING HOPE TO ONE WOMAN, ONE GIRL, ONE COMMUNITY AT A TIME!

Website: www.hopeforherglobal.com

Email: info@hopeforherglobal.com

Telephone:

- **USA (972) 781-8842 (Maria)**
- **Canada (780) 707-0737 (Monica/Maria)**

Notes

11. LET'S DO MORE FOR GIRLS

1. Statistics obtained from https://wwww.girlsnotbrides.org/

Acknowledgments

I would like to extend my most sincere and profound gratitude to all the Co-Authors of the "Beyond the Horizon" Anthology to whom I owe so much respect and more—without you there would be no book.

I want to say thank you for allowing me into your personal spaces and for giving yourselves permission to be vulnerable and gifting the world with your stories. You showed the power that is in our stories. I thank you for embracing each other in your differences in nationalities, religions, cultures and creed. You showed that differences do not separate us but instead they bring us together and we are all connected, and you became the true emblem of sisterhood. For that I salute you and thank you always and forever.

And special Thank you to Ruth Snyder and her RLS Publishing Team —you were the chosen one to be on this journey with us.